THE SHAPE OF
SOTERIOLOGY

THE SHAPE OF SOTERIOLOGY

STUDIES IN THE DOCTRINE OF THE DEATH OF CHRIST

John McIntyre

T&T CLARK
EDINBURGH

T&T CLARK LTD
59 GEORGE STREET
EDINBURGH EH2 2LQ
SCOTLAND

First published 1992
Latest impression 1995

ISBN 0 567 29290 8 PB

British Library Cataloguing-in-Publication Data
A catalogue record for this book is available from the British Library

Typeset by Trinity Typesetting, Edinburgh
Printed and bound in Great Britain by Hartnolls Ltd, Bodmin

CONTENTS

PREFACE

Most books have a flight-path, however long or short, with stops along the way, which provide their own stimulation and yield their own harvest of enriched friendships; and this one is no exception. It began its journey as the Laidlaw Lectures, delivered at Knox College, Toronto, in 1987. From that time, Jan and I remember with affection the kindness of the late Principal, Donald Corbett, and of his wife, Tamiko; all the Faculty who so generously entertained us; and particularly Jamie Laidlaw, a member of the founding family of the Lectureship, who claims ancestral connections with Craigellachie, Banffshire. The next destination was Union Theological Seminary, Richmond, Virginia, 1988, the venue of the Sprunt Lectures, where we were the guests of the President, Dr Hartley Hall IV, and renewed old friendships with Professor John Leith and his wife, Ann, and with members of the Faculty whom we had met on several previous visits. But there was to be further mileage for the Lectures, as they came to form part of the course in Theology, in session 1988-89, for the degrees of BD and MTheol in St Mary's College, St Andrew's University; and in session 1991-92, in New College, the University of Edinburgh, as part of the course known as 'ST2B', the Dogmatics section of second year Systematic Theology. The warmly expressed good wishes of the members of ST2B proved to be a great sustenance and comfort in the illness which overtook me shortly after the end of the course. I had some difficulty in assuring them that the illness was a case of *post hoc,* but definitely not *ergo propter hoc.* From the very varied stop-overs, and from the different reactions to them by the different audiences, it has to be said, the lectures themselves, (and consequently, the eventual book) benefited immensely, so much so that, each time round, they had been amended, one hopes, for the better.

One re-action, which effectively removed any residual immodesty which I might have had in the emptiness consequent upon the completion of the lectures, in a venue not to be specified, was, 'What this [institution] does *not* need is a soteriology!' So perhaps, a word about the title of the book may be in place now. I avoided the use of the obvious word 'atonement' in the main title, although it is the one most widely included in the titles of other books on this subject. I did so because I did not wish to appear to give it prominence over the other models, which I shall be arguing all have to be acknowledged; and have preferred the more neutral word 'soteriology', despite its etymological derivation from the Greek word for 'salvation', and its considerable technical character.

To the Reverend Professor John O'Neill of New College my acknowledgment is due for the meticulous attention he gave to the textual problems I raised with him in connection with I Cor 11.24, though he is not to be held responsible for the views expressed in Chapter 1 concerning the 'Third Order' of Holy Communion in *The Book of Common Order* (1979) of the Church of Scotland.

Finally, to my wife Jan, who has shared most of the flight-path, and seen me through the events of the last year with professional skill, and with so much patience and understanding, I renew my warmest appreciation and thanks.

CHRIST'S DEATH AND OUR REDEMPTION

Anyone approaching the study of the death of Christ, and seeking for a definitive understanding of the classical words of St Paul (I Cor 15.3), 'Christ died for our sins in accordance with the scriptures', encounters an immediate stumbling-block. It is this that the Church has not saught to canonise any specific *theory* of the death of Christ as it strove so earnestly to do with its doctrines of God and of the Trinity, in the Nicaeo-Constantinopolitan Creed, and with its doctrine of the Person of Christ in the Chalcedonian Creed. By contrast, the manner in which the death of Christ, particularly in relation to the forgiveness of sins, is referred to in the credal and later confessional statements of the Church and the Churches is singularly frugal, very varied, and nowhere approaches the sophistication which the doctrines of God and of the Person of Christ achieve at the hands both of the orthodox and the heretical expositors. The point is made twice over by J.N.D.Kelly in *Early Christian Doctrines,* Fifth Edition, London, 1977: 'The development of the Church's ideas about the saving effects of the incarnation was a slow, long drawn-out process. Indeed, while the conviction of redemption through Christ has always been the motive force of Christian faith, no univer-sally accepted definition of the manner of its achievement has been formulated to this day. Thus it is useless to look for any systematic treatment of the doctrine in the popular Christian-ity of the second century' (p.163); and 'The student who seeks to understand the soteriology of the fourth and fifth centuries will be sharply disappointed if he expects to find anything corresponding to the elaborately worked out syntheses which the contemporary theology of the Trinity and the Incarnation presents.' (op.cit., p.375).

The point is of such importance that it merits closer investigation than it has hitherto been given in histories of soteriology; nor has its significance for the assessment of modern soteriologies been always appreciated. Where lies heresy, if there is no defined orthodoxy? The Apostles' Creed makes a good starting-point for our investigation of what some of the major creeds have to say about Christ's death and our redemption. Even if we agree with the dating followed by Professor John H.Leith, *Creeds of the Churches,* Third Edition, John Knox Press, Atlanta, 1983, as c.700, for the Creed in its present form (*op.cit.* p.24), we would still acknowledge as Professor Leith does, that all of its articles individually appear in theological formulae current c.100, and by c.200, they had been compacted into a creed developed in Rome by that date.It is therefore to be taken as reliably reflecting the credal thinking at that time. In the Apostles' Creed, the reference to the death of Christ is a straightforward historical statement, in the second article, 'Jesus Christ, who... was crucified, dead and buried', and it is separated from the belief-affirmation in 'the forgiveness of sins' which comes in the third article. In other words, forgiveness of sins would seem to be more associated with the Holy Spirit, and it is not explicitly related to the death of Christ. That alignment may account for the absence of any interpretation of the death of Christ along soteriological lines, the historical statement being in itself more of an anti-statement negating docetism, offering no substance which might develop subsequently into a soteriology. It is noteworthy that an identical position to that which we have mentioned on the relation of the death of Christ to the forgiveness of sins was explicit in the following: the Creed presented by Marcellus to Julian I (341), as well as what Professor Leith calls 'An African Variant' (*op.cit.*p.25), a credal formula in use in Hippo (c.400), which was apparently known to St Augustine.

The Nicaeo-Constantinopolitan Creed (381) changes direction somewhat, affirming that 'the One Lord Jesus Christ, the only-begotten Son of God ... because of us men and of our salvation came down and was incarnate by the Holy Spirit ... He was crucified for us under Pontius Pilate, and suffered and was buried...' Here, our salvation is presented as the objective of the Incarnation - the Greek *dia*, because of, carrying very little of the representative or substitutionary connotation which we shall discover later in other prepositions used in this connection; whereas, when it refers to 'the remission of sins', it does so in connection with 'one baptism'. The Chalcedonian Creed (451), for its part concerned with the definition of the *person* of Jesus Christ, contents itself with saying that 'in these last days, for us and on behalf of our salvation, [our Lord Jesus Christ] was born of Mary the virgin'. So, again, salvation is mentioned in direct relation to the Incarnation, though no reference is made to the death of Christ or to forgiveness of sins associated with his death. Evidence such as this confirms J.F.Bethune-Baker's long-standing judgment (*Early History of Christian Doctrine,* 1903, reprinted 1962, p.327): '..nothing like a definite theory [of the atonement] is propounded in the earlier ages': 'it was long before any doctrine of the atonement was framed'.

Bethune-Baker is not greatly put out by this circumstance for 'Christians from the earliest days ... did not need to theorise about it; they were content to know and feel it' (*ibid*). However, though there may have been no doctrine of the atonement as such, nevertheless throughout, say, the first four or five centuries, there were statements which went far beyond the sparsity of the credal references to the death of Christ and its relation to the forgiveness of sins. Bethune-Baker made problematic mention of Irenaeus and Origen (*ibid.*) The former is associated with the notion of *recapitulation* (to which we shall later return) which provided an equivalent view of atonement, and some commentators would argue that that exhausts Irenaeus' contribution, or that whatever else he says is subordinate to that. But, Irenaeus does say more, that is not so much subordinate to the *recapitulation* theory as complementary to it, thus: 'Redeeming us by his blood, in accordance with his reasonable nature, he gave himself a ransom for those who had been led into captivity' (*adversus Haereses*, V.1.1); and '... the Lord redeemed us by his blood, and gave his soul for our soul, and his flesh for our bodies, and poured out the Spirit of the Father to bring about the union and communion of God and man. He was able to accomplish this end, paying the price of our salvation, because, recapitulating the full humanity of Adam in himself, he had "real flesh, and blood"' (*id.* V.1.2). Origen, whose theory of the death of Christ as the ransom paid to the Devil for the souls of men was to be influential for centuries to come, nevertheless held other views, derived mainly from Scripture, such as, that Jesus, as head of the body of which we are members, took upon himself our sins, and suffered freely for us; and as a true priest, he offered as a propitiatory sacrifice to the Father, a victim which was himself.

Attention has been paid to the two writers whom Bethune-Baker mentioned with a query as to the extent to which they developed a *theory* of the atonement. But there were many others who, though they had no developed theory of the death of Christ, nevertheless, were much more explicit about the relation of Christ's death to the forgiveness of sins than any of the creeds which we have been considering. Earlier even than Irenaeus, the *Epistle to Diognetus* (c.129?) had declared, against the background of the overflowing kindness and the longsuffering and forbearing love of God toward man, that

God 'gave up his own Son as a ransom for us, the holy one for the unjust, the innocent for the guilty, the righteous one for the unrighteous' (*op.cit.* 9.2). On the other hand, if we move beyond Irenaeus and Origen to Athanasius, who, though so closely associated with the long-lasting theological arguments with a variety of heretics about the *person* of Christ, nevertheless recognised both the importance of the fact of the death of Christ and the nature and purpose of that death. On occasion, as at *Contra Arianos,* 2.61, he seems to be affirming that the redemption of mankind is effected through the Incarnation in itself, thus: '... all men being lost according to the transgression of Adam, His flesh before all others was saved and liberated, as being the Word's Body; and henceforth we, being incorporate with It, are saved after Its pattern'. And yet, in that same work, at 3.31, he unambiguously relates our redemption, through the Incarnation, to the *death* of Christ: 'the Word himself bearing our sins in His body on the tree, we men were redeemed from our own affections, and were filled with the righteousness of the Word'. However, in what E.R.Hardy once called 'Athanasius' B.D. thesis, so to speak' (*Christology of the Later Fathers,* SCM Press, London, 1954, p.46) - the *de Incarnatione* - Athanasius had already made ample use of the biblical descriptions of the death of Christ, notably applying the extended passage of Isaiah 53.3-10 to the interpretation of the meaning of the death of Christ (*op.cit.*34) in answer to the criticism of the Jews. Another interesting point in Athanasius' views on the death of Christ is his use of the notion of 'debts' (*id.*20) in the assertion that the Word, through taking a body was able to die the death that 'must needs be suffered on behalf of all, that the debt owing from all might be paid', an all too brief anticipation of an idea that was to become dominant nearly eight hundred years later in St Anselm. The soteriology of Athanasius is a subject of absorbing interest, and it is already obvious that he uses both a form of Platonic realism to express

the comprehensiveness of Christ's embracing of our humanity, and a range of biblical imagery to convey the effectiveness
of the redemption wrought in the death of the flesh which he
shares with us. We could continue the story onwards, for
example, to St Augustine, who, though he also adopts the
'physical' theory, nevertheless clearly affirms the special place
of the death of Christ in our redemption. Sometimes he may
appear to favour the notion that Christ's blood is the ransom
paid to the Devil for us (*de Trinitate,*13.19); again, he affirms,
following St Paul, IICor5.21: 'Him who knew no sin, Christ,
God made sin, that is, sacrifice for sins, on our behalf, so that
we might be reconciled' (*Enchiridion,*41); and generally
throughout his writings employs descriptions, such as reconciliation, propitiation, expiation, punishment - all of them
part of the biblical vocabulary, as we shall see later - to relate
the death of Christ to our redemption.

So, to recapitulate: one very important point has emerged
from this all too brief review of the best-known creeds and
most outstanding theologians in the first five centuries, on the
subject of the relation of Christ's death to our redemption. It
is that whereas the latter, the theologians, while not producing
a full theory of the atonement, employ a selection of the
biblical expressions to describe the relation between Christ's
death and our salvation from sin, the former are singularly
deficient in their account of the relation, none of them
associating the death of Christ with forgiveness or our salvation, others relating our salvation to the Incarnation, and
another placing forgiveness of sins in the context of the gift of
the Holy Spirit and holy baptism. This circumstance I regard
as being so very, very odd as to merit much more consideration
than it is traditionally given in histories of soteriology; and,
moreover, it has consequences for the later development of the
discipline of soteriology which have been too long ignored.
Bethune-Baker dismisses the matter much too cavalierly in the

comment quoted above (p.3) that the early Christians had such a profound experiential awareness of the atonement secured for them in the death of Christ, that they neither had nor felt any need whatsever to hold, theories on the subject. If it was the case, as he says (*op.cit.*,p.327), that 'the certainty that the life and death of Christ had effected an Atonement between God and man was the very heart and strength of the faith of Christians from earliest days', it is a problem of major magnitude that this certainty and the conviction proved to be no impediment to extensive and sophisticated *christological* statements in the classical creeds over the first five centuries of the Church's life and confessional expression; whereas the certainty and the conviction did not yield similar result in relation to the death of Christ. In fact, Bethune-Baker's 'explanation' of the absence of an adequate soteriology, or even of just an adequate statement about the relation of the death of Christ to our salvation, from the classical creeds, while contemporary theologies carried full statements, albeit of exclusively biblical connotation, serves only to draw attention to the problem, and indeed to emphasise its seriousness. In fact, this 'explanation' leaves us with very fundamental doubts about the relation of the creeds to the actual Christian experience of believers. If a central fact of belief, namely, the close association of the death of Christ with the reality of the forgiveness of sins, is not represented in the creeds, we are left with a choice of two options: either, the biblical writers and the theologians whom we have been quoting have over-stated or even mis-stated their case; or the creeds must be thought of as individually stating sections of the faith, and in this process succeeding in omitting what the biblical writers and major theologians of the first five centuries and later thought to be the heart and ground of the relation of men and women to God. Of the choices, the former is unthinkable, and the latter only achieves credibility, at the cost of serious consequences for all later theology. We must, therefore, look considerably deeper for the reasons for the 'odd circumstance' before us, namely, the absence of a developed theory of the death of Christ, in any way comparable to the Christological theories of the first five or six centuries.

Two such reasons suggest themselves - there may well be more.

The first, and very important reason, for the absence of a full-blown soteriological definition comparable to the Trinitarian and Christological creeds, from the early Canons of the Church, must surely be the centrality not only of a soteriological theme, but of the direct connection between the death of Christ and the forgiveness of sins, to all the *eucharistic liturgies* of the Church. Now it may appear somewhat fool-hardy to attempt to prove or even support any thesis from the vast body of liturgical literature which formed the basis for the worship of churches in Rome, Egypt and Syria, not to mention North Africa, Spain and Gaul, the Balkans and Asia Minor, over the span of the second to the fifth centuries. In addition, there remains lack of documentation on detailed variation, which would form the familiar substance of the day-to-day worship of the people of God, and which, if still available, might well refute the hypotheses concerning the structure of primitive liturgies and their uniformity, favoured by some liturgiologists. Nevertheless, greatly daring, I should like to argue that despite the immense variety of eucharistic liturgy, there lies at the very heart of such liturgy, even if surrounded by other doxological and dogmatic statements embodied in prayers, an interpretation of the meaning of the eucharist which derives from the mind of Christ himself, as contained in the so-called 'institution narrative': as found in ICor 11.23ff, 'the Lord Jesus, the same night in which he was betrayed, took bread: and when he had given thanks, he brake it and said, Take eat: this is my body, which is broken for you: this do in remembrance of me. After the same manner also he took the cup, when he had supped, saying, This cup is the new covenant in my blood (which is poured out for many for the forgiveness of sins, adds Mt26.28): this do ye, as oft as you drink it, in remembrance of me.' Of this association of the bread and the cup with his death, Gregory Dix, (*The Shape of the Liturgy,* Dacre Press, Westminster, Third Impression, 1947, p.77) writes that 'The Messianic, redeeming, sacrificial significance which the whole primitive jewish church unhesitatingly saw, first in His death, and then in His Person and whole action towards God, is the proof that this meaning was grasped by that church primarily through the eucharist, which arose directly out of what he had said and done at the last supper. There, and there alone, He had explicitly *attached* that particular meaning to His own death and office'. Here Dix is echoing almost exactly words of the then Bishop of Derby (1930) in *Mysterium Christi,* ed. G.K.A. Bell, London,1930: 'It was not the death upon Calvary *per se,* but the death upon Calvary as the Last Supper interprets it and gives the clue to its meaning, which constitutes our Lord's sacrifice. The doctrine of sacrifice (and of atonement) was not read *into* the Last Supper; it was read out of it'. Whether we consult the pre-Nicene Roman tradition, as preserved for us in the *Apostolic Tradition* of Hippolytus (and here I acknowledge my indebtedness to the work of Gregory Dix previously referred to), or the Egyptian tradition about the time of the Council of Nicaea , preserved in a manuscript ascribed to Bishop Sarapion of Thmuis, or to the Liturgy of St James, in its Greek or Syrian or Jerusalem forms, or the more semitic Liturgy of SS Addai and Mari - one or other of which, and very probably all, remained influential in the various regions of the Christian Church throughout the whole period when the Creeds were being formulated; the centre of meaning of the whole eucharist is the 'institution narrative', with its clear understanding of the fact and nature of the death of Christ. If, further, we reflect that this understanding of the death of Christ was central to a liturgy practised, not just every Sunday, but more probably every time the congregation met - for the eucharist *was* Christian worship; then we begin to realise that the atonement effected by the death of Christ was more integral to the worship-life of the Church than to the thought-life of its theologians. In a reminder (*op.cit.*, p.12) which we dare never forget, Dix says, the eucharist is 'primarily something *done*, of which what is said is only one incidental constituent part, though of course an essential one'. If the distinction is pressed, it then becomes a category mistake to try to formalise a soteriology, one which the Church avoided for the first four or five centuries, however extensively it committed it thereafter. Moreover, the eucharist is then to be understood as something done not by the ministering clergy exclusively, but by the whole body of the worshipping people, who come to invest the liturgy with fixity of structure, and who conservatively show traditional opposition to alterations in what they have become accustomed to. Here, to my mind, is the reason we have been looking for to explain the absence of proliferation of soteriological theory, to match in any way the sophistication of Christology, particularly in the first five centuries of Christian worship and theology. The understanding of the death of Christ, especially in relation to the forgiveness of human sin, lay at the heart of the eucharist, and the worship which it formed, and the part which it played there defined its role in the life of the church. That role was so articulately defined that there might well appear to be no call to elaborate it farther. Certainly the *plebs Dei* felt themselves to be under no constraint to investigate the matter in theological detail. The connection between the eucharist and the understanding of the salvific power of the death of Christ is an appropriate setting in which to examine a controversial but very significant textual item in the institution-narrative.

The Book of Common Order (1979) of the Church of Scotland, in its so-called 'Third Form', (p.37), in line with several other English speaking denominations, has omitted the word 'broken' from the words accompanying The Action, at the centre of The Communion in the eucharistic office, and uses the form 'This is my body which is for you'. On the previous page, this Third Order has omitted the word 'broken' from the institution-narrative, which it has included in the Great Eucharistic Prayer, but interestingly enough, includes the word 'broken' on the following page (p.38) in the short preface to the offering of the bread to the elders and for distribution to the people. This inconsistency does suggest an uncertainty in the minds of those who drew up this Third Order as to whether the word 'broken' should be included on not. Ambivalence on this point at the centre of the celebration of the sacrament is very confusing indeed for worshippers paying close attention to the details of the service.

It is an Order which I do not normally follow, and I only came upon it some five years ago, when examining the evidence of early liturgies for the understanding of the nature of the atonement. Noticing what I thought to be an omission due to a proof-reader's error, I turned to my Alexander Souter, *Novum Testamentum Graece,* Oxford, 1910), only to find that even then he had dropped the Greek word *klomenon* ('broken) from his text of I Cor 11.24, and has been followed by most subsequent providers of the Greek Text of the New Testament, and not only so, but by almost all the English translations of the twentieth century. Souter and his successors supply notes of the manuscripts which omit and which include the *klomenon*, and indicates options which appear in other manuscripts, such as *thruptomenon* (crushed, broken in fragments), and *didomenon* (given).

The omission or inclusion of the word 'broken' (though, grammatically, we should be speaking of 'being broken') is of such deep significance in the eucharist, that the arguments for and against its inclusion must be carefully considered. The arguments against its inclusion are as follows: 1. First, the weight of credence of the manuscripts favouring exclusion is widely regarded as greater than that of those against, though it has to be observed that the manuscripts favouring inclusion are themselves considerable. It would require an expert to make the decision between them; and clearly that consideration has carried the day, both for the textual critics and, following them, the liturgiologists. But the question is whether the manuscripts of the New Testament texts exhaust the evidence relevant to a decision on the correct reading for I Cor 11.24. 2. There is an agreed principle of textual criticism that when two variant readings, which relate to a single text, differ in degree of difficulty, the more difficult reading has preference over the easier reading. In terms of the logic implicit in this principle, the omission of the *klomenon* (broken) constitutes what is thought to be the more difficult reading; for it is fairly obvious that a scribe would wish to include it (or one of the others mentioned above) in order to complete an original text, which would otherwise be deficient.

There the matter seems to have rested for both the New Testament critics for at least eighty years, but, for their liturgiological followers, for a somewhat shorter time. I have been unable to establish when the omission of the word *broken* first crept into the eucharistic order for English speakers. But I question very seriously whether the matter must be allowed to rest there, despite its apparent conclusiveness, for the following reasons:

1. While it may be comprehensible to say, in English, at the distribution of the elements in the Communion, 'This is my body which is for you' (and 'for you' and 'for you', as the successive communicants receive the sacrament), the Greek sentence looks much more strange, especially when we con-

sider the actual meaning of *hyper hymon* ('on your behalf'); the English 'for you' used in the 1979 *Book of Common Order* would more properly have been the translation of the simple dative, *hymin,* or *eis hymas* ('for you'). In other words, the occurrence of the form *hyper hymon* ('for you', meaning as we have just noted, 'on your behalf') logically, as well as grammatically, implies some such word as 'broken' or 'given'. The term 'difficult reading' is not intended to include actually ungrammatical or even non-sensical reading.

2. On the matter of the 'easy' and the 'difficult' readings, it is hard to see how a textual critic could be satisfied with a reading, whether easy or difficult, which did not make sense. The omission of the *klomenon* or one of its variants, when taken along with the *hyper hymon,* is a syntactical solecism, which has been perpetuated, commonly undetected, because the English translation, 'This is my body which is for you', makes very good sense. But that English sense has to be 'read into' the Greek original to give the Greek form any semblance of sense, and that advantage would be denied the early scribes.

3. But the case for the inclusion of the *klomenon* is even stronger if we look at the matter of the easy/difficult reading from another perspective. It could be argued that in fact it is the *inclusion* of the *klomenon* that constitutes the difficult reading, embodying an intolerable idea for scribes who recalled such texts as Psalm 34.20, 'not one of his bones (i.e., of the righteous one) was broken', echoed in John 19.33, 'but when the soldiers came to Jesus, and saw that he was dead, they did not break his legs'.

4. The texts from which such scribes might have made the omission of the *klomenon* existed in the form of the eucharistic liturgies, which despite local variations, evinced substantial agreements, not least in the matter of the institution narrative and the excerpts from it used in the distribution of the sacrament. It is, therefore, a matter of concern to me that the

textual critics who over the last eighty years have been preparing the definitive text of I Cor 11.24 have not taken into account the very considerable and very early evidence of the liturgies. What surprises me more is that liturgiologists should have seen fit to abandon the incontrovertible evidence of the early liturgies on the inclusion of the *klomenon* in their preparation of forms for modern use, while retaining much else that comes from these liturgies. Faithfulness to the ancient reading, in view of its long-standing at the centre of the eucharist, should, one might have expected, have counted more than an emendation with a slender manuscript majority.

5. Further, there does seem to be something missing when the celebrant lifts up the bread before the people and, breaking the bread, says 'This is my body which is for you'. In fact, it is difficult to see what the 'fraction' now means, with the 'broken' omitted.

6. It is perhaps not altogether fair to make this comment, but it could be said that the omission of the *broken* is particularly acceptable to celebrants and liturgiologists who are not in favour of a substitutionary or even of a representative theory of the atonement. The omission of the *broken* effectively eliminates the view of the death of Christ which has been enshrined at the heart of the eucharist from the earliest days of the Church. Alternatively, the omission of the word *broken* may appeal to extreme Protestants who reject the idea that the bread is 'really' the body of Christ, understood in transubstantiationist terms, and that this body is actually being broken in face of the congregation. Those who support the inclusion of the *broken* need not feel that they are thereby committed to transubstantiationist sacramental theology; the retention of the word *broken* is compatible with other theories of the 'real presence' of Christ in the eucharist.

In a word, omission of the *klomenon* by New Testament critics may be justified on what is thought to be conclusive manuscript evidence and the logic associated with it, though by no means necessarily so; but the omission of the word *broken* from the central parts of the communion in the eucharistic office by liturgiologists with eighteen hundred years and more of eucharistic tradition behind them is little short of liturgical vandalism.

Another possible explanation of the difference in development between Christology and soteriology during the first five or six centuries of the Church's history may lie in the absence of protracted heretical attacks on established soteriological positions, to any degree comparable to the controversies which surrounded trinitarian and christological theories during the third to the fifth centuries. At times we may feel that the sophistication achieved in many of these controversies far exceeds the level of definition required for the expression of a Church's faith. Nevertheless, it has to be acknowledged that the controversies did minister to the growth and clarification of the Church's understanding of the Triune God and of his Son, the Lord Jesus Christ. In much the same way, it was the misrepresentations by the Tropici and the Pneumatomachoi of the nature and work of the Holy Spirit, which induced Athanasius, in writing to Serapion, to correct these errors, by affirming what he saw to be the truth, and so to lay the foundation for the development of a doctrine of the Holy Spirit. But there seems not to have been, during the first five centuries which we are at present considering, any comparable, large-scale attack on the verities concerning the death of Christ and our salvation, which might have elicited a corresponding large-scale response in a developed soteriology.

It is possible to imagine how movement towards greater soteriological articulation might have arisen from the kind of change which Dix (*op.cit.*p.13) contemplated happening to the eucharist. He saw it gradually ceasing to be a rite performed by the whole body of worshippers, and becoming something said by the priest, and what he said and did was said and done on behalf of the people, rather than by the people. Such concentration on the verbalised and representative approach to the eucharist, as distinct from the participatory, would soon lead to the development of the kind of articulated theory concerning the death of Christ, which though it was never to match Christology, was to move down the same road of definition. But it required, or at least, seemed to require actual controversy to bring about the formulation of actual theory of the atonement, and in the subsequent history of theology, such controversy proved to be forthcoming.

So, to demonstrate how controversy and soteriological formulation have gone hand in hand, I propose to look more closely at three points in the history of theology, where this association has appeared. The first occurs with St Anselm who in the *Cur Deus-homo,* allows Boso to confront Anselmus with the difficulties which his fellow-monks and no doubt he himself encounter in traditional soteriological views - in fact, a good case could be made for maintaining that Boso has stated almost all of the difficulties of objectors in subsequent genera- tions. These difficulties include such matters as: would it not have been possible for God simply to forgive the sins of men and women without the suffering of Christ on the cross? Was Christ free to die for mankind, or did his obedience to his Father make his death compulsory for him? Was God obliged to save his creatures to prevent his purposes in creation from being nullified? St Anselm patiently works his way through his answers to these difficulties, and in the end provides the Church with what has been universally regarded as the first systematic account of the doctrine of the death of Jesus Christ. What, however, qualifies St Anselm for recognition as the theologian who formulated the first systematic account of the death of Christ is the sustained nature of his attempt to answer the question contained in the title of his classical work: *Cur*

Deus-homo? why the God-man? Why was it that there had to be a God-man in order that the salvation of mankind should be effected? Why was the God-man so necessary to the scheme of salvation initiated, sustained and fulfilled through the love of God? It is in answering these questions that St Anselm produces a comprehensive work, so distinguished in its handling of a range of issues, in an apologetic style, that it has become a classic in dogmatics. The controversy, the articulate terms of which are spread across the pages of the *Cur Deus-homo?* has occasioned the development of a fully formulated soteriology. In fact, what emerges from this brief consideration of St Anselm and his themes is that the test for any writing on the death of Christ to be considered as a serious presentation of the doctrine of Christ's death, a genuine work in the discipline of soteriology, is whether it tackles the question of the *necessity* of Christ's death. Even Athanasius, who eight hundred years earlier had through controversy done so much to hone the fine edge of Christology, and who as we have seen had much to say on the death of Christ, never faces the question of why it was necessary that the Word, being man, pays for man the sacrifice which fallen man could never pay, and never seriously approaches the question which was to haunt St Anselm, the inescapable quality of the *necessarium* which attached to the death of Christ.

The second occasion of the blossoming of soteriological theory which we shall now consider is the Reformation, which despite its many expressions was fairly uniform in its exploration of the theology of the death of Christ. If the thesis which was argued by Dix that the participation of the ordinary people of the Church in the atonement secured for them in the death of Christ was achieved through the Eucharist, then the late medieval practices against which the Reformation was a protest certainly made such participation ineffectual. Dix, whose interpretation of the Reformed position is far from sympathetic, agrees (*op.cit.*, p.627) that [the Reformers] 'looked out upon a church plagued with a multitude of real superstitions, some gross and wholly evil in their effects, some merely quaint and fanciful, but all equally irrelevant to the christian religion. They had been accumulating for a thousand years ... The existence [of the Reformers] was largely the revenge of the half-assimilated mass of the population upon the church for [their] exclusion from intelligent participation in public worship'. The response of the Reformers to this particular aspect of the very complex situation which occasioned the Reformation was two-fold.

They established, at a very early stage of the Reformation, a liturgy, especially a eucharistic liturgy, in which the congregation could participate. If on the medieval scene, participation in the eucharist consisted in 'seeing', often only for that brief moment in the rite when the host was elevated, the Reformers set out a variety of ways in which worshippers would become involved in the service. An immediate first facility was the offering of a service in the vernacular, the language the people could understand, even when as at Strasbourg from 1524 there were not yet to hand independent Reformed liturgies and translations and adaptations had to be made from Latin to German. (*vide:* William D. Maxwell, *John Knox's Genevan Service Book,* Edinburgh, 1932. This work is somewhat strangely neglected by Dix, *The Shape of the Liturgy,* though Knox's Liturgy, embodying so much as it did of Calvin's liturgical theories and practices as well as his theology, is much more truly representative of the Reformed position on liturgy than R.Baxter, *The Reformed Liturgy,* referred to by Dix, *op.cit.,* pp.608ff. This total disregard, on Dix's part, of all liturgy and liturgiology in Scotland, in this or any century is disappointing in a scholar of such eminence).

Moreover, since the congregation were enabled to understand the various parts of a service in the vernacular, their

participation was greatly extended. For example, in the exhortation delivered by the officiating minister, according to 'The
Order of the Lord's Supper' (Maxwell, *op.cit.,* pp.122-124),
the process of self-examination advised, the invitation extended to the congregation to receive the forgiveness of Christ
through the merits of his death, and the interpretation given
of the meaning of the sacrament of the Lord's Supper, all
together facilitated a high level of participation by the worshippers
in the action of the liturgy. Later, this scripted 'exhortation'
was to be replaced by the sermon, related directly to the theme
of the sacrament, so that it became a tradition in the churches
of the Reformation, that the sacrament was never celebrated
without the preaching of the sermon. Involvement was fur-
thered in two other ways, first, by the attendance of the
congregation at the communion table, and secondly, by their
receiving both the bread and the wine. Here we encounter
another of Dix's caricatures of Reformed liturgical theory,
when he says (*op.cit.,* p.623) that 'there is nothing but a
"figurative" meaning [for Protestants] in such phrases as "to
eat the Body and drink the Blood" of Christ.. At most we are
moved by the tokens or pledges of redemption achieved
centuries ago to rejoice and believe that we *have been* redeemed
long ago on Calvary.' The final misrepresentation comes on
the following page, when Dix affirms that 'In strict necessity
there is no need even of the taking of bread and wine'. These
errors in understanding are made surely in ignorance of the
long-standing prayer in the Presbyterian liturgies, that through
the gift and action of the Holy Spirit, the worshippers, in
receiving the bread and wine, 'may be made partakers of the
body and blood of Christ'. Without labouring the point
farther, we may conclude that the Reformers re-instated a
liturgy in which the congregation participated, to a degree
which Dix regarded as a mark of the worship of the early
church.

We earlier argued that one of the reasons for the absence of a developed soteriology in the early centuries of the Christian era was the centrality of the eucharist to the worship of the church, and therefore to a wide prevalence of the understanding of the nature of the death of Christ implicit in that act of worship. It might appear, therefore, that with the re-instatement of the eucharist, now in the vernacular, and involving as we have seen congregational participation, there was no occasion for farther development of thinking on the nature of the death of Christ. That might have been the case were it not that in the medieval church there had developed a vast theology which formed the theoretical basis for the eucharist as celebrated. It was not enough, therefore, that the Reformers should offer an alternative eucharistic practice; it was required of them that they offer also an alternative soteriology to support the liturgy, and to counteract what were considered errors in medieval thinking on the death of Christ and its relation to our salvation. So four developments took place. One was the formulation of confessional statements, which came to perform several roles in the life and witness of the Reformed church. Chief of these was to set forth to the world where the Reformed church stood on the cardinal elements of the faith, and the doctrine of the death of Christ had a central place in these confessions in all their different expressions. They also fulfilled a normative and regulative role, assisting in the determination of orthodoxy and heterodoxy, so that what they had to say on individual doctrines became prescriptive for most of the Reformed church, and still are even to this day. Now, it could be said, soteriology had criteria for the determining of truth and falsehood in statements about the death of Christ, as Christology had had for some eleven hundred years. The second development followed from the first and was the formulation of catechisms, summarising and essentiating the great doctrines of the confessions. By this method of teaching, and it was not confined to children, for adults also were regularly catechised and duly examined, there was built up a definitive, if not very greatly elaborated, conception of the theological background to the explicit, acted soteriology of the eucharist. It is interesting to observe that this penchant for formulating confessions was not confined to the Reformed church. The Council of Trent, first convened by the Roman Catholic church, in 1543 and continuing until 1563, produced in its Canons and Decrees a document very similar in form and themes, however differently treated, to many of the Reformed confessions. Thirdly, in the grand manner there were written theologies, systematically setting forth the Reformed understanding of the faith, with very notable contributions to soteriology, for example, by John Calvin in his *Institutio*. These underpinned the confessions, the catechisms, and also the liturgies, and particularly the eucharistic liturgies, of the national churches of the Reformation. Fourthly, the pressure for a school for every parish, such as was Knox's dream for Scotland, led within a generation to a heightening of the general educational level, and consequently, to a greater ability to understand the articulate theology of catechism, confession, sermon and text-book. Given the central emphasis on the atonement in the eucharist and in Reformed theology, it was not surprising that as a doctrine it should in that period acquire a definition and immensity of coverage, such as it had never previously had in the history of the church. So, our argument has been that both the decline in the understanding of the central significance of the eucharist, and what was considered to be an unacceptable interpretation of the nature of Christ's death and the believer's participation in it, constituted the catalytic conditions for the articulate, normative and prescriptive definition of soteriology in the Reformed church.

To conclude: whatever variations we may go on to encounter in the shaping of different soteriologies, these variations, if they are to remain within the limits of Christian connotation, will be founded upon these twin facts - the historicity and particularity of the death of Christ and the integral relationship between Christ's death and the forgiveness of our sins. The variations in soteriology, the conditions and sources of which we now go on to consider, may be traced in large part to the different ways in which theologians have described the relationship between Christ's death, as a very particular event which really happened, and our salvation. Without agreement on the fact of that relationship, on the precise nature of which they differ, there could be no soteriology as we know it in the Christian faith.

We mentioned earlier that we would choose three points in the history of doctrine where, it seemed, the substance of the doctrine of the death of Christ was developed in reaction to circumstances which called in question certain aspects of it. We have examined two cases of such reaction, one by St Anselm, and the other by the Reformers. Just as the events which we have been examining in relation to the Reformers covered a considerable period - confessions were being written at least from mid-sixteenth century to mid-seventh century - in much the same way the circumstances stimulating a re-definition of soteriological subjects in our third example cover a similar stretch from the nineteenth into the twentieth century. If it were possible to give a single name to the catalytic agent in this case it would be :the ethicising of the attributes of God. In classical historical theology, the attributes of God are so presented that the metaphysical, transcendental attributes - 'bloodless categories', as they have on occasion been called - receive a dominant place, or are so positioned as to limit the character of the others. Omniscience, omnipotence, omnipresence, unity, infinity, eternity, transcendence, and immanence, together offer a rather formidable front to the more moral, as we might call them, attributes such as love, mercy, goodness and justice. Such a doctrine of the attributes of God had for centuries been partnered with a fairly strictly structured doctrine of the atonement, which spoke in strongly biblical terms of the propitiation of God and the sacrifice of Christ on calvary for the sins of the whole world. Another feature of this traditional account of the attributes of God which I have been describing is that the different attributes are conceived of as being independent of one another, there being no interpenetration of one by the other. Against such a background, the doctrine of the atonement as traditionally presented appeared to many to be setting the love of God over against the justice of God, and such opposition was enough in itself to create renewed soteriological analysis.

So, the real instigator of such analysis was the realisation of the fact that the attributes of God are not to be regarded as isolable from one another. Not only are they mutually dependent, they interpenetrate one another, and influence one another. The late Principal John Baillie used in lectures to say that there are some of the attributes of God which qualify the others, and he would mention specifically infinity and eternity; though once you start to think along these lines, as I have argued elsewhere, the theorem could be applied to other of the attributes, notably love and mercy. It might be thought to be a process of mutual limitation, whereas in fact it is one of mutual enrichment and deepening. Inevitably, such a central event in the dealings of God with his people as the death of Christ was profoundly involved in this theological process, and in being so, in its turn, exerted a powerful influence on the understanding of the attributes of God.

A further contributor to what I have been calling the ethicising of the attributes of God has been the perception of the 'I-thou' character of God's relationship to ourselves, which was the inspiration of Martin Buber, whose book *Ich und Du* was first published in 1923, and translated into English in

1937 as *I and Thou* (T.&T. Clark, Edinburgh). The translator, the late Professor R. Gregor Smith, said somewhat prophetically in the 'Translator's Introduction' (*op.cit.* p.v), that '*I and Thou* will rank as one of the epoch-making books of this generation'. Its insights have been incorporated in the writings of every great theologian in the past sixty years. The soteriological categories were now given a personalised quality, or perhaps more precisely, that quality which had always been present was now made explicit. A process which had its beginning in McLeod Campbell's *The Nature of the Atonement* (1856) reached its fruition in the concluding chapter of Colin Gunton's distinguished *The Actuality of the Atonement* (1988) entitled 'The Community of Reconciliation', so named 'because it is hoped in it to show how the reconciliation between God and the world achieved on the cross may take shape in a God-given community ordered to that purpose' (p.177). The years between these two dates saw the publication of writings on the significance of the death of Christ, which were charcterised by the two emphases which I have mentioned, the ethicising and the personalising of theological and consequently, soteriological, categories.

So a century and a half which has produced in Britain, not to mention Europe where corresponding examples exist, some fifty works in the field of soteriology has also witnessed great controversy and disagreement, thus illustrating our theme that controversy promotes articulation, and in this case, also variety. Compared with the first five centuries, this modern period is no better-off in the matter of credal definition and precision, and the immense variety just mentioned may result somewhat from that continuing lack, if so it be. On the other hand, it is much better-off in another respect. For, while the theologians of the early centuries elaborated the connection between the death of Christ and God's forgiveness of human sin, such elaboration never amounted to the provision of a *theory* of the atonement. Theology had to wait until St Anselm for that. Modern theology has followed in his footsteps, and what we have been given is an almost overwhelming plethora of different theories, apparently at odds with one another, sometimes even based upon an analysis of the defects of the others. There is, however, one respect in which these different theories are similar to one another, and this circumstance constitutes a second interesting feature of soteriology, the first being the absence, already noted, of any credal definition of the significance of Christ's death, or of its relation to human sin. To this second feature of soteriology, the similarity in difference of the apparently heterogeneous theories of the atonement, we now turn.

2

THE MODELS OF SOTERIOLOGY

Introduction
We concluded the last chapter with the comment that despite
the variety of soteriological theory, particularly in the nineteenth and twentieth centuries, this variety had one distin-
guishing feature, and it constitutes a second respect in which
the history of soteriology differs from that of christology. On
the one hand, we are aware that the models of christology
comprise a very rich mixture not only of biblical terms, such as,
Son of Man, Son of God, Jesus, Christ, the Lamb of God, and
so on, but also certain metaphysical terms originating in Greek
philosophy, such as *hypostasis* and *physis*, enshrined in the
Chalcedonian creed, and all its variants and deviants. This
mixture has been further enhanced in modern times through
the addition of concepts derived from such philosophies as
existentialism and process, and such system-builders as Tillich
('New Being') and Teilhard de Chardin ('omega point'). So,
on the other hand, when we turn to examine soteriology in a
similar way, we are not quite prepared for the fact that, by
contrast, the images, figures, concepts, metaphors or, as I shall
prefer to call them, 'models' (for reasons to be discussed later)
are almost all exclusively *biblical* in character and origin. What
we have witnessed in the history of the Church's thinking
about the death of Christ has been the quite remarkable
capacity on the part of such models to root themselves in a vast
variety of heterogeneous cultures, and to find comprehensible

expression in generations separated from one another sometimes by hundreds of years - and that fact is no less true today
than it was 400 or 1500 years ago. That circumstance is for me
one of the most intriguing problems, or enigmas, about
soteriology, the significance of which has received scant
consideration in studies of the atonement.

I intend to enumerate and discuss as comprehensive a range
as I can muster, of the models which have been employed by
New Testament scholars, as well as by theologians and preach-
ers, to expound and develop the Church's understanding of
the nature and significance of the death of Christ. The main
part of the presentation will be the New Testament terms in
their standard translation, supplemented by Old Testament
associations, together with soteriological variations which
emerge from alternative translations. Thereafter, to complete
the muster, we shall consider any models that fall outwith the
New Testament provision.

Such deployment will serve a two-fold purpose. The short-
term interest will be to see what the options have been and still
are for those who wish to write on the atonement. Mention has
already been made of how such writers not only elaborate
positive accounts of the subject which they themselves
support, but also of how they take great pains to dissociate
themselves from other positions in the list. It is not unfair to
say that most soteriological theories contain a major anti-
theory component, as if the positive theory gained strength
from the destruction of its counterpart. Obviously it is not
going to be possible to be totally unprejudiced even in the
compiling of such a list, especially when it includes commentary
on the options; but the risk is one which has to be taken in the
interests of comprehensiveness, in order to do justice to the
negative-positive, or even the love-hate, character of much
soteriological writing. The longer term intention of such
comprehensiveness of presentation is to develop the claim that

they are *all* germane, however sometimes partially, to the full understanding of the nature of the death of Christ, and by implication to the mediation of the forgiveness which that death has secured for God's people. If it is the case, as has been maintained, that the models of soteriology seem to have the capacity to revive themselves in cultures and contexts vastly different from those in which they originated, then it is unwise at any point in the history of the Church to 'write off', or in any way disregard, models which have served the cause of interpreting the death of Christ to believers in earlier generations. Perhaps it is a pity that so much theology tends to be of the 'either-or' variety, owing a great deal to the influence of Kierkegaard upon twentieth century theology, and so little is of the 'both-and' character. So much of the former, once its protest has been made, requires the balance of the latter in order to secure the truth in its fulness. If the term 'inclusive' had not been pre-empted for one kind of theology and theological language, I would at this point have been making a plea for an inclusive treatment of the theories of the atonement, and shall, in any case, be arguing for the retention of the models of soteriology in their comprehensiveness. They form, as it were, a catena from which the Church may find itself compelled to draw at any given time, or in specially emerging circumstances. So, if we resist the highly selective procedure followed by many writers on soteriology, adopting some one or other of the models, and arguing against others, and if with a contrary logic we hold to the idea of a catena of models, we shall have to offer some understanding of how the models are related to one another and to the event and significance of the death of Christ. But first, we must attend to the roll-call of the models, remembering that we are dealing with English terminology, even though it is related to a range of Old Testament and New Testament source-words.

The Models

1. We begin with the notion of *ransom*, and in doing so we are carrying the examination of the previous chapter into the understanding of the relationship of Christ's death to the forgiveness of sins one stage farther. In that chapter, we were considering how that relationship was conceived of in the creeds, confessions and liturgies of the Church over many centuries. Now, I would venture to claim, we are in touch with our Lord's expression of what he thought about his own death.

The *locus classicus* for the application of the model of ransom to the death of Christ is, of course, Mt20.28=Mk10.45: '...the Son of Man came not to be served but to serve, and to give his life a ransom for many'. Modern criticism, largely inspired by Bultmann, has argued that this theme has its roots less in the mind and spirit of Jesus than in the theology of the post-resurrection community, who in their tradition assigned it to Jesus in retrospect. I shall, however, consider how Pannenberg, writing in *Jesus: God and Man,* (ET, SCM Press, London, 1968, pp.247ff) and who is no Bultmannian, nevertheless treats the ransom text along similar lines, thus:

1. He assimilates it to I Cor 15.3 : '... Christ died for our sins in accordance with the scriptures'; 2. which, because it is Pauline, is to be associated with the post-resurrection community. 3. Next, he affirms that the Pauline passage does not depend on Is 52.13 - 53.12; and 4. that consequently, neither does the 'ransom' passage, despite the fact that *prima facie* the passage does have strong affinities with Is 52.13 - 53.12. Pannenberg then proposes to adopt as the original form of the 'ransom' saying, which he would ascribe to 'Jesus' messianic consciousness', the simple statement in Lk 22.27b, where Jesus says, 'I am among you as one that serves'. The saying is then reduced to an emphasis by Jesus on his servant role exercised in deepest humility, without any reference to ransoming sinners or any eschatological overtones in the use of the phrase 'the Son of Man'.

I find several grounds for resisting this process of erosion. First, the late Professor Manson, in his exceptionally scholarly *Jesus the Messiah,* (Hodder and Stoughton, London, 1944. p.132), suggests that while the *form* of the word 'ransom' may be admitted to have a post-resurrection ring to it, and he adds that the case is not a strong one, yet even that admission does not itself prove that the *idea* contained in it was not original to Jesus. I would want to go even farther and say that the connection between the 'ransom' saying and the Servant Song of Is 52.13 - 53.12 is direct and not mediated through St Paul or the community. In fact, there is considerable textual evidence drawn fron the Psalms, Isaiah and the inter-testamental literature, (*vide* W.Manson *op.cit.,* pp.132ff) to bear out the association of propitiatory death with the redemption of the guilty, thus to form the proper context in which to understand the 'ransom' saying. So what I wish to hold is that the association of the death of Christ with ransom, sacrifice and redemption, was not only endemic to the thought of the post-resurrection community concerning the death of Christ, which few even of the sceptics would deny, but also that this association had its inspiration in the mind of Jesus, as he employed an emerging tradition, which had already begun to link the suffering of the martyrs with the redemption of God's people, in order to understand and interpret his own mission and death.

Let me make two general comments upon the 'ransom' model. First, it did not have an altogether unfaltering history in the thought of the Church, as theologians, with a natural thirst for logic, began to ask: to whom was the ransom paid? By the time of Origen, the answer being given was: to the Devil; but it was Gregory of Nyssa, who expressed this position in now classical terms, in what must surely go into the Guinness Record Book as the first theological joke. Beginning from the presumption that mankind must have become slaves in bond-

age to Satan, Gregory argues that God, in order to recover his
own, plays a trick on Satan, by offering his own Son incarnate
and humiliated, the ransom. Satan is completely deceived by
this ruse, failing to perceive that 'the deity was hidden under
the veil of nature, that so, as is done by greedy fish, the hook
of Deity might be gulped down along with the bait of flesh
(*Oratio Catechetica Magna* 22). The Deity thus ingested
vanquished darkness and death in the devil's domain, and thus
accomplished the recovery of mankind to freedom and life. It
was a theme which was to re-appear frequently (as HD
McDonald points out in *The Atonement of the Death of Christ*,
pp.143ff.), for example, in Gregory the Great and Peter
Lombard. On the other hand, it was an answer which was
equally forcefully rejected by a series of major theologians,
notably, Cyril of Alexandria, John of Damascus, St Anselm
and Abelard. Both Cyril and John allowed that the devil had
dominion over mankind, whereas St Anselm, followed almost
literally by Abelard, will not allow that the devil has any right
to claim possession of mankind, because 'the devil and man
belong to God alone, and neither one stands outside God's
power' (*Cur Deus-homo,I*.8). This post-biblical history of the
model, 'ransom', serves to illustrate an important point about
how models are to be employed in soteriology: they are not to
be implemented totally literally, as if they were 'complete
symbols' of the death of Christ, but rather as 'incomplete
symbols', which require us to desist before pressing them to
their logical conclusions.

Secondly, an equally important feature of these models is
also already in evidence. In dealing with the 'ransom' text (Mt
20.28=Mk 10.45), we noticed that the notion is not properly
understood in political, transactional or commercial terms of
buying someone off; but requires for its exposition the central
soteriological notions of sacrifice and expiation. But by drawing on these others we have run ahead of ourselves, for we have

still to examine them as we have done the 'ransom' model. The signal is that we dare not isolate them from one another, or regard them as in competition with one another.

2. I have selected as our second model for consideration, that of *redemption*, which has become almost the universally accepted interpreter of what was effected by the death of Christ. Innumerable biblical texts come to mind, for example, Eph 1.7,14 and Col 1.14. There is very little linguistic justification for drawing mutually exclusivist differences between the words translated as 'redemption', namely, *lutrosis* and *apolutrosis*, on the one hand, and on the other, the word which we have just been discussing at length, namely, ransom (*lutron*). Accordingly, we might be tempted to say that we should take no notice of the difference between ransom and redemption. I can not quite agree. English usage, sharpened by 380 years of usage of the King James Version, has established a certain differentiation between the notions of ransom and redemption, with 'ransom' retaining much more of its etymological origins and their overtones than 'redemption', which has been able to some extent to control if not to eliminate the idea of buying back and has come to be dominated by the soteriological content, and often to be used comprehensively for that content. But there is, it has to be confessed, a residual element of the notion of 'buying back', perhaps not, this time, from whom? but certainly, from what? So the answer is not, on this occasion, from the devil, with the freedom from embarrassment which that answer, as we saw, has caused, but rather from the power of sin and death. Even here there is a degree of personification, as sin and death were almost persons who had to be bought off, to enable the recovery of sinful mankind, and to set them free to love and obey God. But in fact the personification does not rise above the level of metaphor, and certainly does not reach the point of personalisation. Nevertheless, once again the edges of the model are uneven, for God

is under obligation to pay no one and no power to recover the creatures who are his own in the first place and always. Moreover, it is extremely difficult to imagine the death of Christ as in any sense a payment or a purchase : what is *given*, and what is *received* in return? So we register that this model is an 'incomplete symbol', which we can not complete without distortion of that which it is intended to describe.

3. A third model which pervades not only almost all the biblical talk about the death of Christ, and God's purpose revealed therein, but gathers up the whole of God's will for his people as we are given to understand it throughout the entire history of the people of Israel, is the model of salvation and its variant forms. The biblical texts are numerous, and they include the verb form , 'save', the concept, 'salvation', and the name, 'Saviour' applied to Jesus on the basis of his saving work. ('Save' -Mt1.21; I Ti 1.15; Heb 5.5; 'Salvation' - Ac 4.12; Rom 1.16; Heb 5.9; 'Saviour' - Jo 4.42; Titus 1.4; II Pet 1.11). Comparing this model with those which have gone before, we may discern certain similarities and also some differences. 3.1 For example, once again the question could be asked: saved from what? and the answer would be given in the Pauline terms of: from the wrath of God, which is aroused by the sin of men and women who have broken his commandments and are in a state of rebellion against him, saved also from the power of sin and death and the Law (Rom 5.9). This time, however, there is not present even the suppressed reference to payment, or the suggestion that the power of sin and death and the Law is in any sense personal. 3.2 Next, there is beginning to emerge a prospective element in the way in which the death of Christ is to be interpreted. For, not only does that death save *from* sin and death and the Law, but also *for* a life forgiven, life everlasting and a whole new range of wholesome relationships, especially involving obedience to God. It is at this point of our soteriology that we ought to be alert to the importance of the

doctrine of the Holy Spirit, who as Christ's gift to his saved and redeemed people initiates and sustains these relationships within a whole new life. 3.3 Finally, we observe that the Greek word for 'salvation', *soteria*, provides for us the standard term for the branch of theology that we are examining, namely, soteriology. Unlike the two previous models, and several of the others which are yet to be considered, the model of salvation comes very close to being a 'complete symbol', with little if anything of its content being reducible to metaphor, or if taken literally, leading to distortion of the message of the model. In fact, I would prefer to see this model employed as the definitive term, particularly because of its completeness, for the study of the death of Christ, rather than that of 'atonement' which is favoured recently by HD McDonald, in the work quoted, and several years ago, in an equally comprehensive book, by TH Hughes, *The Atonement*, London, 1949. What we have witnessed has been a single model with specific associations and connotations acquiring a generic function, or at least a classificatory role, so that even accounts of the death of Christ which contain elements that are foreign to the idea of salvation as such have come to be classed as soteriological theories.

4. We come now to a cluster of models, which while closely related remain nevertheless distinguishable from one another. They all have strong connections with the Old Testament, and the most important of them, and in some ways the control, is the model of 'sacrifice'. The writer of the Epistle to the Hebrews antithesises at great length the sacrificial system of the old covenant, according to which the priests and high priest offer a constantly recurring and incomplete sacrifice with the once-for-all sacrifice of Christ who offered up himself. (*vide* Heb.5-10 *et passim*). Many of the purposes of sacrifice which Frances M Young (*Sacrifice and the Death of Christ*, 1974) itemises are applicable to the death of Christ ; to cleanse the worshipper from unrighteousness; to seal a covenant; to be an

offering to God, in which first of all Christ offers himself, and in which subsequently the worshipper may also participate; to establish communion between God and those who worshipped him. As these different themes are developed in the Epistle to the Hebrews, the prospective feature of the model, which we observed in examining the model of salvation, becomes increasingly evident. For that sacrifice once-for-all has become the basis of the whole future relationship of God and his people. Now there is sitting at the right hand of the Father one who constantly makes intercession for his own (Heb 6.25). He also has given to them the gift of the Holy Spirit as the foundation, the context and the inspiration of the new sanctified life that God's people are going to live.

5. Some of the subjects which we have encountered in considering the model of sacrifice re-appear under the next model, namely, propitiation, which occurs classically at I Jo 2.2:(KJV) 'Jesus Christ the righteous... is the propitiation for our sins; and not for ours only, but also for the sins of the whole world'. (cf I Jo 4.10; Rom 3.25 KJV). There are therefore not many biblical references, but the prevalence of this way of describing the death of Christ arises from its being part and parcel of the sacrifice model, describing what is entailed or effected by the self-sacrifice of Christ. The term has dropped out of almost all of the modern translations of the Bible, largely it might be supposed because the original associations of the term appear to be too harsh and unacceptable, suggesting as they do, the angry God whose wrath has to be placated before he can overlook the wrongdoings of sinners, and to achieve this end exacts the blood of the innocent victim. There is then created, so it is thought, a rather intractable problem in apologetics, namely, of reconciling the love of God with his wrath. The problem has been dealt with at two levels - the linguistic and the theological.

5.1 The simplest, if least satisfactory, way of dealing with the problem is - if I may be allowed the allusion - to change the goal-posts by offering alternative translations for *hilasmos* (propitiation). For example, the NEB, in translating I Jo 2.2 and 4.10, speaks of Jesus as 'the remedy for the defilement of our sins'. Still farther removed from the original Greek is the translation offered by the *Good News Bible*, which refers to Christ himself as 'the means by which our sins are forgiven'. In the event, therefore, neither of these translations is particularly helpful as regards the problem from which we started; for the first gives us no inkling of how 'the remedy for the defilement of our sins' works, while the second has nothing to say about what the means are which Jesus employs to effect the forgiveness of our sins. The ideology of sacrifice and propitiation may be thought crude in some ways, and even to savour of early Jewish religion, but it does provide some insight into how forgiveness is achieved and into the supreme costliness of it. In fact, these other notions of 'the remedy for our defilement' and 'the means of our forgiveness' only have meaning and content insofar as they presuppose something of the notions of sacrifice and propitiation which they set out to exorcise. They are parasitic upon the basic biblical models, and belong to second-order thinking. When you reflect upon such so-called translations as we have been examining of what must surely be one of the most central notions in the whole of Christian theology, we might be moved to ask the questions: when is a translation, a translation, and when is it a paraphrase? How much licence should a translator be allowed, so that he can re-write the Bible? These questions are posed in a very immediate way in the present climate of multiple translations, which sometimes in the name of seeking communicability actually misrepresent what the Bible said. Sometimes too, theological considerations are introduced to give the text what is thought to be a more acceptable meaning. Considering these basic biblical models a little farther, we might be inclined to say that their effectiveness as soteriological descriptions derives from their capacity as explanations of how forgiveness works. Some of the variant translations which we have been reviewing err on the side of offering descriptions, and fall short on explanation. For that reason, there is a sense in which every account of the death of Christ is an attempt to answer within the human limits possible, the question, why did Jesus Christ die?

5.2 I mentioned that the apologetic problem set by the biblical use of the term 'propitiation' to describe the death of Christ, just because it seems to carry an overtone of suggestion that an angry God has to be placated, has been handled both linguistically and theologically. We turn now to the latter device. We shall look briefly at two possibilities, which are offered in *A Dictionary of Christian Theology,* 1969, ed Alan Richardson, art. 'Atonement', by James Atkinson (incidentally a much better article than that on the same subject in *A New Dictionary of Christian Theology,* 1983 ed Alan Richardson and John Bowden, and written by FW Dillistone). Atkinson proposes on the one hand that though God remains throughout the whole redemptive process as the God of infinite and all-encompassing love, sinners experience this love as wrath. Their sin can not but produce a negative re-action from God if God is to remain all-righteous. The fact that God's love is not extinguished is evidenced in his decision to initiate the redemption, rather than the annihilation, of the sinner; and the death of Christ effects both the redemption of sinners and the propitiation of the wrath of God. It was a position which had been argued with great persuasion over forty years earlier by Emil Brunner in *The Mediator,* German 1927, ET 1934, when he spoke of God being 'angry' (ET pp. 478ff) and of God being the only one who can make the sacrifice to cover human guilt. On the other hand, it is suggested in the article by Atkinson, that since the universe which God governs is moral in character, the moral law must be honoured. There is a close relation between sin and the retribution which is its due. Christ is the bearer and the sufferer of that retribution, even when his acceptance of it, even unto death, derives from the love of God for sinners, and from his own love for them. At this point it appears that the apologia for the model of propitiation has transgressed its own boundaries to employ the legal model, as we have seen previous models also re-inforcing and to some extent explaining one another. (Attention might be drawn to H.Bushnell, *The Vicarious Sacrifice,* 1881, Part III, which long ago used the concept of law to expound the full character of sacrifice).

6. The attempt is sometimes made to avoid what is thought to be unacceptable elements in the model of 'propitiation' by shifting the accent slightly to give the model of 'expiation'. I might have mentioned it earlier when we were discussing the ways in which translators endeavour to avoid some of the nuances of the original language by bland translations, but 'expiation' is itself so clearly a soteriological model in its own right, that it deserves separate treatment. The connection with the earlier discussion is nevertheless important, for 'expiation' does not appear in the classical New Testament soteriological texts as appearing in the KJV, whereas it replaces 'propitiation' in the RSV. The words that we are speaking of in the Greek are *hilasterion* (Rom 3.25) and *hilasmos*(IJo2.2 & 4.10) with the kindred verb, *hilaskomai.* I have in our previous discussion been indicating a case for the firm position on 'propitiation', but views of commentators are so varied that it would be wrong to be inflexible. CH Dodd, for example, argues straightforwardly for 'expiation' as being the proper translation. My main reluctance to give in wholly to the 'expiation' lobby is that the two models are slightly different and carry different references. 'Propitiation' has a God-ward reference, which admittedly comes with its etymology in classical Greek, but which theo-

logically answers to an important element in the soteriological situation, which is expressed in all the statements about Christ's self-offering to the Father, about the sacrifice of the only-begotten Son, about Christ's making our peace with the Father - all so central that they can not be wiped away by equating propitiation pejoratively with appeasement of an angry God.

On the other hand, the word 'expiation' has a more manward reference, carrying the meaning of 'reparation' or 'amends', and implies retrospection to wrongs done, or sins committed, with the result that the guilt is extinguished and forgiveness secured. The difference that I have in mind between 'expiation' and 'propitiation' can be best brought in the two verb forms, which show that we speak of 'propitiating God', but of 'expiating our sins and their guilt'. These cases, in both of which we are speaking of the action of Christ on the cross, both therefore carry the connotation of great pain and suffering, and in that respect there is no distinction to be drawn between them. Perhaps, then, the outcome is to affirm the necessity of both 'propitiation' and 'expiation' in the shaping up of our soteriology, on the grounds that the two models are saying things that are different, and without either of which our doctrine would be less than complete.

7. To continue within the circle of ideas associated with sacrifice, we proceed to the model of 'atonement', which by 1970 had not appeared in any of the modern translations, and is literally not a NT way of describing the death of Christ, occurring only once in the KJV at Rom 5.11 . Yet it has so established itself as to have become the generic name for the doctrine of the death of Christ, embracing all the others. Of course, the Hebrew word for 'atone', *kpr*, occurs many times in the OT, and it is associated centrally with the sacrificial ritual. Originally the word meant 'to cover', and so to cover the person or his/her guilt from the eyes and the judgment of the

all-holy God, thus to procure his/her forgiveness. The atoning virtue was thought to reside in the blood of the victim. As we have noted, in the NT KJV at Rom 5.11 'atonement' appears as the translation of *katallage*, which the NEB like the RSV translates as 'reconciliation' (which incidentally Liddell and Scott gives as the appropriate translation, including no reference whatsoever to 'atonement'), as does the KJV on the other occasions when the term occurs (Rom 11.15, II Cor 5.18f) with its variants - *katallasso, apokatallatto, diallattomai*. Yet despite this single occurrence, this *hapax legomenon,* of 'atonement' in the KJV, I still would favour holding it as one of the models for describing the death of Christ. For, in addition to being very much a part of the circle which includes 'propitiation' and 'expiation', it establishes continuity with the OT range of ideas concerning sacrifice which re-appear so unmistakeably in the NT, in the record and the liturgy of the Last Supper, in the whole image of the new covenant, in the constantly recurring references to the blood of Christ in almost every one of the Epistles and Revelation. I do not know what other word quite so effectively comprehends that vast compass of notions and ideas, and so despite its lack of NT linguistic documentation, I would judge the argument to be strong for its retention. That is said in full recognition of the considerable weight of support for the view - and it is an undeniably accurate view - that these passages with the *allasso* based verbs must normally be translated as some form of 'reconcile'. Nevertheless, the notion of 'reconciliation' is different from 'atonement', and can not be offered as a comprehensive substitute, however linguistically and etymologically validated, for what is intended by the term 'atonement'. To lose the latter is to lose a major section, as we have seen, of what the NT has to say - and we have to add, what the Church in its subsequent thinking has to say - about the meaning of the death of Christ.

8. We have several times now referred to what must be one

of the most important of the biblical models for describing the death of Christ, and also one which has considerable influence with our contemporaries, namely, 'reconciliation'. The reconciliation of sinners with God is effected through the death of Christ, and that connection, which we previously maintained to be one of the incontestable convictions of the Christian faith, is always present, as the texts of St Paul amply verify. Rom 5.10 'For...while we were enemies we were reconciled to God by the death of God's Son'. cf. Eph 2.15; Col 1.20-22. Let us comment briefly on this model:

8.1 First, and very significantly, the NT nowhere says that God has to be reconciled to us; but we are to be reconciled to him. Now there is no question of an angry God having to be placated. On the other hand, there is now the temptation to think that all that takes place in the act of reconciliation is a change of heart in those who have been estranged and alienated from God. That certainly has to take place, and it does as part of the whole reconciling activity of God in Jesus Christ, which is designed precisely to make good the alienation between God and mankind, created by human sin. The relation between the two has been damaged, distorted even disintegrated, and if we are serious about the dimension of the alienation, it is difficult to avoid the conclusion that it affects God as well. The anthropomorphism of the phrase 'the wrath of God' was certainly trying to put words to this effect of his alienation from mankind upon God, but it has to be re-affirmed that when such language occurs along with reference to our being 'reconciled to God by the death of Christ', as at Rom 5.9f., it occurs in the context of St Paul's words, 'God shows his love for us in that while we were yet sinners Christ died for us' (Rom 5.8). Estrangement and alienation there may be on God's side, yet it does not cloud or detract from God's love for sinners, which pours itself forth in the gift of his Son on the cross. So, II Cor 5.20 'be ye reconciled to God' does not mean 'change your attitude to God', but rather 'enter into the new relationship which God has in his love created for you through the death of his Son'. The change of heart and of attitude will be created through admission to that new relationship, the new life in Christ.

8.2 Secondly, we dare not omit to recognise the popularity of this particular model in contemporary theology, particularly because it can be stated in person-to-person terms. Because of its close association with what I have been calling the circle of sacrifice, it carries substantial salvific content, containing both the objective and the subjective elements which are integral to valid soteriological theory. When, however, it is extended to other fields of personal relationship, for example, in the area of ethics, the original use of the term remains as the norm - a claim that should not be reduced in times when the tendency is so often to allow the secular use of a term to become normative even for Christian ethics. Notice is then taken of the facts that reconciliation is often, if not always, at great cost to someone, usually the person offended and wronged, that reconciliation is effected when he/she takes the initiative to heal the breach, and the offender is the one who is in this process reconciled.

9. A further model, but one which does not fit in to the pattern which has been developing, is associated with the name of Gustav Aulen set out in his *Christus Victor*, 1931. He calls it the 'classic idea', and it consists of several clear and simple affirmations: the salvation of mankind is a divine conflict and victory in which Jesus Christ on the cross triumphs over the evil powers of this world and of this age, 'tyrants' under which mankind has been kept in perpetual bondage and suffering ever since the Fall. The atonement is a cosmic drama of salvation in which God in Christ reconciles the world to himself. The context of this view is dualistic, not in a metaphysical way, as in manicheism or zoroastrianism, but

nonetheless in a radical way which sees these powers of evil as viciously hostile to God and all his purposes for mankind and the world. This work of atonement is presented as being from start to finish the continuous work of God and of God alone, not partly God's work and partly man's. Aulen claims that the 'classic theory' is the dominant idea in the NT, being at the foundation of ransom theories, and the ruling soteriology of the first thousand years of the Church's history. He finds his view illustrated chiefly in Irenaeus and Luther, but castigates most of the remainder of writers on the death of Christ down the centuries, as allowing a place to man in the process of victory over evil which belongs only to God.

Three comments may be made : 9.1 The sponsoring text for this theory is Col 2.14f: '(God) cancelled the bond which stood against us with its legal demands, nailing it to the cross. He disarmed the principalities and powers and made a public example of them, triumphing over them in him'. Now the model reflects much else that is said in the NT about the death of Christ, yet it is inaccurate to give the 'classic theory' such pre-eminence, especially when it relies on several of the others for its actual complete statement. It is a case of a brilliant idea being over-stated. (Cf. the excellent critique of Aulen in Colin E. Gunton, *The Actuality of the Atonement*, pp. 53ff.) 9.2 Nor does Aulen serve his own purpose well by being so - I almost said, 'defamatory', and that would not be unfair - prejudiced in his assessments of those who have written on the atonement across the years. He is on a number of occasions actually wrong. 9.3 As to his main thesis, it has to be observed that in the history of doctrine, it has been when the death of Christ has been taken together with the resurrection that the theme of 'Christus Victor' is most frequently and dramatically pro-claimed. In fact the Colossians passage which is so important for Aulen (2.14f) is preceded by references to the readers being 'buried with Christ in baptism'and 'being raised with him through faith in the working of God, who raised him from the dead'. It is a false abstraction to separate crucifixion from resurrection as Aulen does, almost in neglect of Scripture.

10. We come now to the tenth of the soteriological models for consideration, namely, punishment or penalty. It is a model which has been central to the soteriology of theologians across the ages, and for those of us in the Reformed tradition, in the thought of Calvin and Knox, and more recently, in the writing of Emil Brunner. Brunner's assessment of the importance of this model is given in the following words, (from *The Mediator,* E.T., Lutterworth, London, 1937, p. 455): 'Two series of statements of a parabolic nature determine the scriptural message concerning the fact of the atonement: firstly, the parables which deal with the payment of debts, which are taken from the practice of law, with their ideas of penalty and satisfaction; and secondly, analogies drawn from the practice of the cultus, with their emphasis upon the sacrifice and the shedding of blood. Both merge into one in the idea of expiation...' We have already considered the different models that nucleate around the notion of sacrifice, and while there is strong *prima facie* support for a view that sacrifice and penalty are not to be separated off from one another, the latter providing an essential element in the interpretation of the former, it is excessive to say, as Brunner does, that 'Both merge into one in the idea of expiation'. Not only is expiation, as we have seen, only one of several models in the sacrifice nucleus; but I have also to say that the biblical status of the idea of punishment is not immediately self-evident. For example, I can not find New Testament statements which outrightly affirm that the death of Christ was a punishment visited upon Jesus rather than upon the mass of sinful mankind. However, it is not difficult to see how, if several texts are taken together, the death of Christ may be so described. For example, we have all along made the claim that Isaiah 52.13 - 53.12 has a central

place in the understanding of the death of Christ, not least because it seems to have been very influential in Jesus' self-understanding; e.g., 53.5 'He was wounded for our transgressions, he was bruised for our iniquities' could scarcely be more explicit on the punitive nature of the death of the Suffering Servant. But there is also similar New Testament evidence. If we interpret II Cor 5.21 'For [God] made him to be sin who knew no sin' in the light of the other text 'The wages of sin is death' (Rom 6.23), we come very close to the statement that Christ died the death which was punishment for sins, but these sins were not his own, but theirs, the brothers' and sisters', against whom their trespasses should properly have been counted.

This model has long been the victim of caricature, the God of whom it speaks being construed as a bloodthirsty oriental monarch, or some deity of primal anthropology, whose whims and caprices have to be cajoled. The very mention of punishment in relation to sin, it is sometimes suggested, is redolent of 'the primitive instinct for revenge' (Brunner, *op.cit.,* p. 468) So much of this caricature has been accepted in so many soteriologies of the nineteenth and twentieth centuries, whether it has been inspired by philosophical idealism or by presuppositions which have their roots in the Enlightenment, that the time has come to take a definitive stand for the fundamental truths about the death of Christ which it enshrines. For example, the model takes its start from the absolute sovereignty of God, the fact that God is God, a deep awareness of the holiness of God, set over against the sinfulness of men and women, and the awful gulf of guilt that that sin sets between them and the righteous God. It recognises that, in a universe in which the will of God is paramount, sin, as disobedience to God and violation of his will, merits punishment, which if dispensed in an appropriate measure would result ultimately in the destruction of the sinner. It is only when we grasp the total seriousness of that possible and properly moral result, that we appreciate the overwhelming quality of God's love which comes to us in the likeness of human sinful flesh, to pay the price, bear the penalty and in so doing to overcome the gulf of alienation between himself and his sinning creatures. In transcending the Law, as Brunner argues (*op.cit.,* p. 475), and so showing his own freedom over it, God in Christ 'intensifies the validity of the Law as absolute' (*ibid.*) The Cross then becomes the medium through which the absolute holiness and the absolute love of God are revealed simultaneously. 'The Good Shepherd lays down his life for his sheep': this is the essence of righteous love.

11. The next soteriological model for consideration is *satisfaction,* and it is difficult here not to begin by reference to St Anselm's definitive employment of the term in what is generally recognised as the first comprehensive treatment of the death of Christ in the history of theology, his *Cur Deus-homo,* written 1096-98. He uses the term in a quite special way. Because God requires from all of his creatures total obedience, their sin in disobeying God places them in a position of total inability to make good their alienation from God. This process of 'making good' the broken relationship with God St. Anselm calls 'satisfaction', and it involves both perfect obedience to God's will and reparation for the dishonour done to God in disobeying him in the first place. So, while man is the one who should make satisfaction for the sin committed, insofar as he committed it; on the other hand, God is the only one who by reason of his perfectly righteous nature could possibly and competently make such satisfaction. So the *Deus-homo* is the one who completely fulfils these requirements. Hence, out of the infinity of his love for his creatures, and to prevent the perversion of the original purpose of his creation of mankind, and to maintain what St Anselm called 'the order and beauty of the universe', God sent his Son to earth, the *God-man.* He

made adequate satisfaction, both in his total obedience to the will of God and in making amends for the dishonour done to God in the original disobedience committed by mankind. In this way the *God-man* achieved the salvation of those for whose sakes he was made flesh.

We have to wait, however, almost eight hundred years for the expression of another form of satisfaction which reflects a growing tendency to emphasise the moral and spiritual features of the atonement and to minimise what were thought to be the legalistic and commercial elements in previous accounts of it. The pioneer of this tendency was J McLeod Campbell whose work, *The Nature of the Atonement,* 1856, is a classic. The model unfolds in the following way. God is eternally willing and ready to forgive human sin, wherever sinners are fully repentant and make adequate confession of their wrongdoing. Because of the depth of its involvement in sin and guilt, mankind is utterly incompetent to meet such an absolute demand. Accordingly, Jesus Christ in the active outgoing of sacrificial love and in full apprehension of God's wrath against sin, responds by taking the nature, and becoming the brother, of those whose sins he confesses before God the Father. In so doing, he offers a perfect and equivalent repentance, in sorrow and contrition, as a true, proper and vicarious satisfaction to God's righteousness and offended justice, thus securing for mankind God's full forgiveness. In expounding his theory, McLeod Campbell makes use of certain of the other models we have encountered, such as, atonement, redemption, propitiation and expiation.

But he stedfastly refuses to use the model of punishment, denying that Christ's death is a penal infliction visited upon him as the substitute for sinful mankind (*op.cit.,* p. 146). His reason for this denial is that to describe Christ's death as 'penal', when in fact he is wholly righteous, is to employ an unacceptable fiction. Two replies are possible to this claim.

The first is that it is an equal fiction to speak of vicarious penitence, insofar as Jesus can not feel the shame which the sinner feels over his disobedience in the manner in which the sinner feels it. The second answer is that McLeod Campbell is here encountering an aspect of the soteriological models which we have ourselves frequently noted, namely, that they can not be applied totally literally to the description of the death of Christ. It becomes interesting when we link this rejection of a penal theory to St Anselm's well-known phrase, *aut poena aut satisfactio*, 'either punishment or satisfaction'. By this phrase St Anselm seems to imply that the notion of punishment defines the judgment which God will impose upon mankind for their sins, provided, and only provided, some other way is not opened up of making amends to him for the dishonour done to him by human disobedience. He holds to this disjunction, either punishment or satisfaction, so consistently that he nowhere describes the death of Christ as penal in character. It may be that St Anselm senses the same difficulty as McLeod Campbell felt, namely, that punishment was appropriate only to wrongdoers. What St Anselm and McLeod Campbell would both accept is that the satisfaction, as they differently describe it, is both God's condemnation of human disobedience and his forgiveness of it. Nevertheless, it would appear that there is a character endemic to satisfaction theories, even when they are separated by close to eight hundred years of theological reflection, which entails their rejection of the model of punishment. But perhaps they would, each in his own way, have an answer to that implied criticism, namely, that the notion of punishment is not excised from their systems, but that, through the love of God for sinners in the death of Christ, it is transformed, for St Anselm, through the satisfaction offered by the *Deus-homo,* and for McLeod Campbell, through the vicarious pentitence which he experiences and expresses.

12. There is a another model, namely, example, which is treated by some theologians as a model in its own right, and by the majority as capable of use along with some of the others which we have enumerated. There are three difficulties about 'example' being a first order model for the description of the death of Christ. One is that the death of Christ is only an example if we first define what its nature in itself is, so that what is to be imitated then becomes clear. That definition will involve one or other of the other models in our list, so that the example model is dependent on one of the others, and insufficient in itself. The second difficulty in taking example as a first order model is that it presupposes that mankind has the moral and spiritual ability to imitate the example of Jesus Christ. But the absence of such ability in mankind is the very circumstance which made atonement a necessity in the first place. And thirdly, an example as such is not necessarily redemptive. In fact, quite the reverse, for the perfect obedience of one man to the will of God, in spite of the sufferings entailed by such obedience, might show up human disobedience in an even worse light than it would be without such an example.

In parenthesis, we may note that similar qualifications would have to be made if it were proposed that 'revelation' be regarded as another soteriological model. It could only be so considered if it also were definitely regarded as a second-order model. Thus, the death of Christ can be said to 'reveal' the love of God, or God's redemptive purposes for mankind, only if, in the first place, Christ's death has been described in terms of one of the other models in our main list, for example, as sacrifice, or atonement, or victory. There are two points of interest here. The first is that in any case there is virtually no biblical evidence for regarding 'revelation' as a soteriological model, worthy to be ranked along with the others we have examined, nor has it established itself in the history of doctrine. In the second place, this circumstance is somewhat of an enigma, when it is remembered that 'revelation' has been one of the most popular christological categories of twentieth century theology, despite, once again, its absence from the biblical descriptions of the person of Christ, and from the historical credal or confessional definitions of his person. In short, 'revelation' christology has failed to produce a comparable soteriological model, being obliged, as we see from the writings of Barth, Brunner, Bultmann and the many others who employ it so extensively, to fall back on the traditional models enumerated earlier.

Returning to the 'example' model, which is to be regarded, as was said, as a second-order model, we find that there is convincing evidence for taking it in that way, when imitation is considered as a response to the central significance of Christ's death. The biblical classical case is Philippians 2.5-11, which opens with the words, 'Let this mind be in you which was also in Christ Jesus our Lord' and later, at verse 8, 'who being found in human form humbled himself and became obedient unto death, even the death of the cross'. But there are other instances: Mk 10.39 '... Jesus said to James and John, "The cup that I drink you will drink; and with the baptism with which I am baptized, you will be baptized."' Again, we have Jesus' words to the multitude, 'If any man will come after me, let him ... take up his cross and follow me' so anticipating Christ's own death. In the opening verses of Hebrews 12, the author after exhorting us to run with patience the race that is set before us, looking unto Jesus, who endured the cross, invites us to consider him who endured such hostility against himself. His example is our inspiration. There is no doubt that the notion of example is a clear biblical theme, and it is associated, as we have seen, in all the cases mentioned, with the death of Christ. But I have to conclude that we can not regard it as a soteriological model standing, as it were, on its own feet. What Jesus does in his death is exemplary for us essentially because of his total obedience to the Father's will, but it is an example which we

can only begin to consider, because of the redemption which
he has won for us through that obedience, and once again only
through the enabling power of the Holy Spirit.

13. Before leaving the models, it would be wrong to make
no reference to Liberation Theology, which is sourced so
deeply in both classical christology and soteriology. It might
appear that there is a *prima facie* case for regarding 'liberation'
as itself a further model in our list. It has become a dynamic
key-concept around which a whole range of ideas cluster, but
it is by no means simply an ideology or a philosophy. It is a
theological praxis, which in the 'seventies of the present
century transformed the Church's understanding, in both its
Catholic and its Protestant phases, of the Christian's responsibility for, and involvement with, the poor and the
underprivileged of the world. But more, it stimulated, height-
ened and energised the Christian conscience world-wide, and
few Christian denominations have failed to respond to its
promptings. Yet despite the essentially practical implications
and impact, I feel compelled to regard it as a model also.
Admittedly it does not have the comprehensively inclusive
New Testament documentation of some of the earlier models,
and indeed much of the biblical material which it employs, and
employs so persuasively, is drawn from the Old Testament.
Two specific New Testament text are I Cor 7.23: 'ye were
bought with a price; do not become slaves of men'; and Rom
6.23: 'For the wages of sin is death, but the free gift of God is
eternal life.' So the claim to regard 'liberation' as a model does
not rest upon its direct documentation in the Bible, which does
not speak literally of the death of Christ being a 'liberator'. Its
claim rests rather upon its capacity to employ the many other
models which we have been considering - ransom, sacrifice,
propitiation, atonement, salvation, victory and so on - and to
integrate them into a dynamic unity, which creatively and
imaginatively inspires both praxis and theoria. Of 'the notion

of liberation', Gutierrez writes, 'it is a complex, differentiated unity, which has within it several levels of meaning which are not to be confused: economic, social and political liberation; liberation which leads to the creation of a new man in a new society of solidarity; and liberation from sin and entrance into communion with God and with all men' (*A Theology of Liberation,* ET, London, 1974/1979, p.235). Nevertheless, despite the comprehensive economic, political and social sweep of the liberation model, as its supporters expand it, its anchoring in soteriology is secure, for in a discussion of the Eucharist, in which we 'celebrate the cross and resurrection of Christ, his Passover from death to life, our passing from sin to grace', Gutierrez declares, 'Liberation from sin is at the root of political liberation. The former reveals what is really involved in the latter'. (id.,p.263) There could be no more convincing refutation of the charge that Liberation Theology is marxist in inspiration.

We have come now to the end of the review of the soteriological models and it has borne out our initial claim that writers on the death of Christ have made their selection from a fairly firmly controlled list, which draws its sources almost exclusively from the Bible. We have observed, too, that however much as purists we may wish to abide solely by the soteriological words as they occur in the original texts of the Old and New Testaments, we are obliged to take into account variations in the translations of these words which, in turn, have given rise to different models and different theories. To that extent, we have made a beginning to meet the challenge of Yves Congar (*Masses Ouvrieres,* No.259, Dec.1969) when he wrote, 'It is necessary to ask ourselves again very seriously about our idea of salvation. There is hardly any other theological notion implying immediate consequences - very concrete and very important - which has been left so vague and calls in a most urgent way for an adequate elaboration'.

3

THE LOGIC OF THE MODELS

The review of the models of soteriology which we have just completed is the point at which so many theological studies of the death of Christ both begin and end, these models being thought to be all that is required for the definition of the theories of the death of Christ, and their enumeration being regarded as forming the sum-total of soteriological analysis. But if we are to pursue such analysis to the degree of elaboration which Congar desiderated, several steps remain to be taken. We shall begin by asking two questions, which arise as soon as we reflect upon these models, not so much in terms of their individual emphases, and of the respects in which they differ from one another as we have so far been doing, as in respect of the logic under which they all operate insofar as they hold a place in soteriology. The first question is: how are these models related to one another? The second is: how are they collectively related to the death of Christ, the event which they describe, and which they are designed to communicate to us?

I.

How are the models related to one another? Though it is not a question which is extensively examined in studies of soteriology, it follows very naturally upon the consideration of the variety of the models. In the event it is quite surprising to discover just how many the possibilities are, and the very proliferation of them will help to extend our understanding of

53

the quite special role that the models play in the process of salvation. The following suggest themselves as ways in which the relations of the models to one another may be presented: 1. Let us begin with *pluralism*, which is at present enjoying considerable popularity. Until recently the term had been reserved for the description of the variety of religions which have come to be domiciled in western society, or alternatively, while inhabiting the wider confines of the 'global village', have acquired, through the media of press and television, a publicity unimagined even twenty-five years ago. In this context the term has been thought to provide an exit from all obligation to make discriminatory judgments concerning the possible validity or truth which such religions might contain. Now, on the other hand, it has found its way into Christian theology itself, still possessed of its previous franchise from discrimination and truth-judgments, and armed in addition with an invitation to disaffected theological factions to practise peaceful co-existence. Quite apart from the question why truth and peace should, rather than, as the Psalmist says, be kissing one another, actually be, if not in conflict with one another, then divorced from one another; quite apart also from the question whether we can long hope to preserve social and racial peace by pretending that religious differences do not matter, or that religions do not make truth-claims which may ultimately be in conflict; nevertheless, doubts must now be certainly be raised about the credibility of applying the bland category of pluralism to the present near chaotic state of theological differences.

Nevertheless, while the pluralistic thesis might not be generally applicable to theology, perhaps a case could be made for its adoption in soteriology, where certain circumstances give it a *prima facie* plausibility. In particular, the clear-cut lines of the several models which we have just been examining would at least suggest that these are so many different and differentiated ways of describing the death of Christ. If you are more at home with a sacrificial model, you elaborate your soteriology in one way; if a judicial type of thinking seems to be more adequate, you adopt that; and so on with such models as reconciliation, atonement, satisfaction and so on. But the relevance of the pluralistic thesis to soteriology and its several models, to my mind, ends at that point, for this reason that the thesis implies four characteristics which can not be extended to cover soteriological models.

1.1 The first is conflict. The world-faiths confront one another in an attitude of contradiction and mutual rejection, which sometimes spills over into active and violent aggression, but which is almost always subliminally present on the intellectual level. In fact, it was precisely because this conflict and contradiction had become so intolerable, and so much in violation of many of the individual faiths themselves, that the pluralistic formula proved to be so attractive. But, though it does occasionally happen, mostly I fear in theological societies, that there are openly outspoken differences of opinion between supporters of different soteriologies, the relationship never approaches what could remotely be called 'aggression'.

1.2 The second characteristic of entities in the pluralistic category is that they should make mutually exclusive truth-claims. It is at this point that the presuppositions of the entire nineteenth century missionary enterprise has been called in question by certain exponents of latter-day missiology, who on occasion go as far as to suggest the suppression of the classical texts in Ac 4.12 : 'For there is no other name under heaven given among men by which we must be saved'; and in Jo 14.6: 'No one comes to the Father, but by me' - both because of their overtly exclusivist expressions. Such missiological, compromising pseudo-apologetic I regard as a waste of time, for two reasons: one, such exclusivist statements are not unique to Christianity, but can be paralleled in almost every major religion. So, even if Christianity were willing to modify its claims, it would be doubtful whether other faiths would be equally accommodating. Two, such exclusivist statements are the expression of the total commitment which each religionist makes to the subject of his/her belief, and which does not allow for the possibility that an equal commitment might be made to some other Ultimate Reality. Neither Agrippa's ambivalence 'Almost thou persuadest me to be a Christian' (Ac 26.28) nor St Augustine's 'Lord, make me a Christian, but not yet' is a paradigm of faithful commitment in any religion. But it is that exclusivism, so central to the relationships of faiths to one another, which would disqualify pluralism as a method of describing the relations of the soteriological models to one another.

1.3 A third feature of pluralism prominent in entities it is used to characterise is independence. Sometimes, in relation to world-faiths, this feature is minimised, if not even denied, by philosophers of religion who endeavour to find comprehensive categories, within which the dissimilarities among religions may be homogenised, the religions themselves presented as instances of one universal. Such procedure, tidy as it may be for metaphysics and for philosophy of religion, is a denial of pluralism, which rests upon the absolute differences of the plural subjects. There is, therefore, a contradiction in much present-day religious studies, in that an attempt is made both to hold to the pluralist thesis and yet to try to find a common genus or common genera under which to subsume the world-faiths. As we ourselves have already observed, there is not very much independence among the soteriological models. On the contrary, they penetrate one another, and assist one another in their self-presentation and understanding.

1.4 There is one other major difference between the models of soteriology and those of the world-faiths, namely, the former all relate to a single identical, historically verified subject, while, as regards the latter, on the contrary, it is an outstanding ground for disagreement whether the world-faiths have as their single subject, the one identical Person, or Ultimate Reality. It has been frequently argued that such is the case, but it is far from proved that there is unity of ultimste subject of worship in the faiths. Pluralism affirms that there is not, and so far as soteriology occupies the opposite stance, it can not be defined in pluralistic terms.

2. Before pluralism became the popular panacea for theological disagreements which it is today, there existed what was in fact a much more plausible form of it, in the guise of *historical relativism*. Applied to soteriology, it means that the different models, which have been employed to describe the death of Christ are congruent with the culture within which they were first presented, the assumption being that this congruence would facilitate the appropriation by contemporary hearers of the Gospel message. A cultural context of this sort would, of course, itself be complex, embodying social values, moral standards, previously held religious beliefs or myths, memories of the nation's or the community's history, its expectations for the future, and so on. It was a theme which was, now many years ago, employed with his customary flare by the late Charles Raven (as I mentioned in *On the Love of God,* London, 1964, pp.124ff) in lectures on the Island of Iona to the Community. Ransom, he argued, made a great deal of sense to a slave group, who longed for nothing more than the day when they would be bought for a price and released - a model which has come to enjoy a new lease of life in liberation theologies, for that same reason. We might add, he did not, that a culture dominated by a belief in ethereal beings, both demonic and good, would welcome news of the conquest of the evil spirits, the 'principalities and powers' and 'the spiritual hosts of wickedness in the heavenly places' of which St Paul speaks in Eph 6.12 - the conquest of which Aulen writes in *Christus Victor.* A religious community brought up on the

cultus of the old Israel would readily carry over the sacrificial concepts to the understanding of the death of Christ, re-inforced as it was, with the description of Jesus as the Lamb of God. In feudal times, when duties had to be performed for the overlord, and reparation made for duties unfulfilled, 'satisfaction' inevitably chimed in with medieval social and economic thinking. In the theological climate in which Raven was arguing his case, it had a certain persuasiveness, especially when it was made the premise for an almost evangelical appeal to the Iona Community to go out and find the appropriate symbol or image - we were not talking about 'models' in those days! - which would fulfil the role which successfully communicant media had achieved in other ages.

Despite the rather attractive form which Raven gave to what we now see was an expression of historical relativism, and the obvious uses to which we might put it in a not too sophisticated account of the atonement; nevertheless, as a serious account of how the different models of soteriology may be said to be related to one another, it is not beyond criticism. For example, in claiming that truth, historical truth or soteriological truth, is proportioned to the context in which it occurs, relativism comes close to affirming that the content of the truth is contextually conditioned. Treated even less kindly, relativism could be charged with saying that truth is communicability. As Mr McLuhan so famously said, 'The medium is the message'. If this form of relativism were really the truth, it would be difficult to understand how so many different generations with such vastly different cultural backgrounds should have succeeded in understanding models of soteriology which were drawn from contexts so alien to their own. Moreover, if we were to respond to Raven's invitation to go out and find the appropriate model for our generation, what criterion would we employ to assess the truth or falsehood of our presentation? It would not be enough, *pace* McLuhan, that our contemporaries should apprehend what we were saying to them. The history of the doctrine of the work of Christ is strewn with attempts to popularise the doctrine, which have turned out to be fallacious. So without the availability of some norm by which to judge the valid from the invalid in soteriology, it is hard to see how we could have ever have been able to separate the false from the true, or the orthodox from the heretical, in the doctrine of the atonement. This circumstance is made all the more embarrassing by the absence from soteriology of any credal definition, comparable to the chalcedonian creed, which has proved to be so influential in christology. Yet there does seem to be some implicit norm or other which enables such discrimination between what Barth once referred to in relation to proclamation, as 'that which must be said under all circumstances and that which may be said under none'. Historical relativism, even of the near-acceptable kind promoted by Raven, leaves us with a vacuum at the very point where we most need guidance. So we have to carry forward from this discussion of the historical relativist's account of the relation of the soteriological models to one another, the question of whether such an account presupposes for its adequate working the existence of something like an absolute and definitive understanding of the death of Christ. Otherwise, how could we ever be sure that the salvation achieved within the ransom culture was effectively the same as that offered within a sacrificial system.

Before leaving the historical relativist theory, let me mention one aspect distinct from those which I have been mentioning and in which all cohere. We noted that in that theory the context in which a certain model was able to thrive, or as some might even say, in which a certain model was generated, was determinative of the content, structure and comprehensibility of the account of the death of Christ which was developed from it. That assumption I would want to challenge. It savours too much of that pre-understanding which the existentialists sometimes require of those who hear the Gospel, if they are to have any hope of receiving it as the Good News. In the latter connection, we have to reply that it is the role of the Gospel to call in question all human pre-understanding; besides, there is no justification for proposing that there can be any human pre-condition for receiving the Gospel, other than the presence of God's Spirit. Equally, the soteriological models may question the very contexts which are thought to support them, as I think we have seen happening. The sacrifice who offers himself for the salvation of his sisters and brothers revolutionises the whole understanding of sacrifice as it had obtained for centuries in the Jewish system. The infinite love with which a just God meets the demands of justice through the gift of his only Son, to save the sinners who have disobeyed him, in that single action transforms the meaning of justice in fulfilling it, and throws a whole new light on how justice and love are related to one another. The meaning of the death of Christ so construed could never have been conjured out of any social context or set of moral values, obtaining at the time of the Primitive Church or indeed since. In a sense, it is that transforming quality of the events of the atonement which is at least a part of what we have in mind when we speak of its being revelatory of God's inmost being. Had it been the product of social conditions, we would have been in an entirely different order of thought.

3. We shall consider in somewhat briefer terms a series of further ways of attempting to describe the relationship of the models of soteriology to one another. For example, an obvious possibility is to employ the notion of *complementarity*. Much has been made of this notion in theology, but for our purpose it may be sufficient to look at two forms which it has taken. The first is the scientific form which appears in, for example, the two views of the nature of light - as corpuscular and as

undulatory - in light theory as we used to be taught it. Under certain circumstances light evinces qualities appropriate to corpuscles, and under other circumstances, those appropriate to waves, but there is no higher formula under which the two systems of description may be comprehended. Now this form of complementarity has been employed from time to time in theology, and it has been helpful in a number of areas. I would not adopt it myself, but I could imagine someone applying it in christology, and saying that we may speak of Jesus Christ in terms of the divine attributes which he shares with the Father, and in terms of the human attributes which make him one with ourselves. But beyond affirming that these two sets of attributes reside in what theology calls 'one Person' - very much as scientists are speaking of one phenomenon, namely, light, which they describe in terms of waves and of corpuscles - there is no higher genus within which the two natures may be subsumed. Complementarity, interpreted in the rigorous scientific sense, has also been applied to the compresence of freedom and necessity to human behaviour, for while there is a clear case for saying that freedom is the distinctive condition of activity which is human and moral - 'I ought implies I can' is a lesson that is not readily forgotten or gainsaid; nevertheless, human activity can be described in terms of a closed network of natural law and necessity. Again, it has been argued, there is no common denominator within which the freedom and the necessity may be comprehended, though both series of descriptions are required to do full justice to the single phe-nomenon, namely, human activity. But complementarity of that sort is exactly not applicable to the description of the death of Christ, for, as we have ourselves seen, the different models and the descriptions which they facilitate inter-penetrate one another, some of them occasionally relying on the others for their final implementation. In fact, one of the unsatisfactory features of the history of soteriology has been the way in which too little trouble has been taken to spearate the models from one another, with a view to examining how they have influenced one another. That it has been possible to do so demonstrates the inapplicability of the complementarity concept to the models of soteriology.

It will be recalled that complementarity might be considered in a popular as opposed to a properly scientific sense. In ordinary parlance, it would mean that the several models supplement one another and among them provide a comprehensive picture of the inner meaning of the death of Christ. What is not affirmed in one view is supplied in another. This theory is interesting as far as it goes, but perhaps its very generality counts against our being able to use it for the settling of certain questions that it itself raises. For example, is it proposed that the models, particularly those which we have listed as being classical, among them exhaust the field, or is there room for yet further models to be adopted? If new models appear, on the other hand, must they be shown to be derivative from the classical instances we have noted? It is difficult if not unwise, to suggest that the canon of soteriological models has been closed; and the unwisdom arises from the fact that the existence of definitive biblical models in christology did not prevent the emergence of non-biblical models which subsequently became normative. So why not also in soteriology, even although the church has had centuries to produce such non-biblical norms for soteriology and has not done so? Another form of this difficulty is that normally when two statements are said to be complementary, it is implied that between them they exhaust the field. I am not so sure that those who want to say that the soteriological models are complementary fully believe that these models are exhaustive in this sense. In short complementarity is not a wholly adequate concept for our purpose of describing the relation of the soteriological models to one another.

4. Another concept which is employed in both a popular and a specialist sense to describe the relations of models of the death of Christ to one another is that of *dimensionality*. Popularly construed, it is tolerably acceptable, suggesting as it does, that there are different levels at which we may regard the death of Christ, some of them more profound than others. Dimensions are by definition higher and lower, but few supporters of this view go so far as to arrange the different soteriological models in that kind of hierarchy. Mostly, those who select one model as more important than the others tend to use that one to the exclusion of the others, which is a virtual denial of the dimensionality concept according to which the higher gathers up the lower to make it part of itself.

It was, however, the late Professor Daniel Lamont, himself a physicist, who taught several generations of students at New College, Edinburgh, a true appreciation of dimensionality and its place in theology. He defined (*vide Christ and the World of Thought,* Edinburgh, 1935, pp.64ff.) a dimension as a field within which distinctions of one particular order are drawn, or relations of one particular kind obtain, for example, the three spatial dimensions, or the five sensory dimensions of seeing, hearing and so on, such dimensions occurring within familial groupings. He went on to direct our attention to the three characteristics of dimensions. One is independence, which is the recognition that relationships and qualities which exist on one dimension are peculiar to that dimension and are not reducible to any which obtain on any other dimension. Independence so defined is not to be confused with the independence discussed in the context of 'pluralism', where it was equated with isolation and incompatibility. A second characteristic of dimensions, according to Lamont, is polarity, which extends the significance of independence, and applies it to entities which, while independent, imply one another, as, for example, the outside and the inside of a cup, or up and down, or the North Pole and the South Pole. A third characteristic of dimensions is paradox; an event or character explicable from the level of one dimension is paradoxical when viewed from another - someone acquainted with only two dimensions finds it paradoxical that a cow depicted on a canvas as ten times the size of another is in fact the same size as the other, the difference in size being interpreted three-dimensionally to indicate that the apparently larger cow is the nearer. Lamont's listing was on his own showing incomplete; for he had earlier pointed to, and included in his own illustrations, the characteristic of dimensions which I shall call familiality, the quality of residing in familial groups. The spatial dimensions exist in a group, as do the sensory dimensions, a problem which greatly exercised Aristotle in his *de Anima* in relation to the senses.

The application of this notion of dimensionality to the description of the relations of the models of soteriology to one another seems to have a certain validity. There is a certain self-sufficiency of the models, which is Lamont's understanding of what he calls their independence of one another. We can explore their meanings separately, as some theologians have done, to the exclusion of others. Yet, the truth must surely lie in taking independence with polarity, so that co-implicative relationships can be demonstrated to exist between different models. The language of 'objective' and 'subjective' is only permissible when understood in terms of polarity. Paradox, it seems to me, runs all the way through the models generally - as we see in the paradoxes of love and justice, of mercy and judgment, of the God who has been sinned against himself providing the sacrifice, of the Sinless One dying for the sins of the sinners. Familiality is the concept that gathers together comprehensively the variety of the dimensions, the different models, so that together they contribute to the richness of the whole.

5. There are three other possible accounts of how the models in their relatedness may be described, which I shall mention

briefly. 5.1 First is *perspectivism,* the idea that the models constitute perspectives along which we may view the death of Christ. If you stand in the perspective of the Jewish system of sacrifice, as St Paul's Hebrew readers and listeners would have done, it is inevitable that you will be drawn to think of Jesus' death in such terms; in much the same way as, it is said, St John the Evangelist presented the person of Christ as Logos to men and women whose perspective was that of Greek philosophy. Such a view is in effect a variant of pluralism, with a different origination, but it gives no indication of how the perspectives are to be related, or of how we determine the validity of a perspective.

5.2 Secondly, there is what you may consider the mysterious *'centripetal axial reference'* theory of the inter-relations of the models. The image is that of a wheel with a hub at its centre and the various spokes of the wheel pointing towards that centre, and the hub itself being on an axle to which another wheel may be affixed, by means of a hub. The theories of the death of Christ are centripetally directed to that event, which is not to be identified with any of them, but which lies in the direction in which they all point. The different models of the New Testament, which in the main we have considered, would form the spokes of one wheel; and it is conceivable that other theories, should we succeed in formulating them, would be centripetally related to another hub on another wheel. So long as that hub remained co-axial with the hub of the original wheel, and its spokes pointed to the centre on that same axis, then these other theories could be regarded as new models for the development of new theories about the death of Christ. Personally, I would regard such a view as too ingenious by half, and useful only if employed in the most general terms.

5.3 Thirdly, I would like to use a notion associated with the name of Gadamer, but to develop it in a manner with which he would not be identified. I refer to his concept of *horizons.*

The theories of the death of Christ could be regarded as providing so many horizons which intersect at that point which is the death of Christ. Each of us may stand within the area of which any given horizon is the boundary, and looking in the right direction we may glimpse the cross of Christ. If, however, culturally, the cross itself should lie beyond the horizon of the areas in which we normally move and think, it may just be possible that one of our horizons extends to a point of intersection with one of the areas defined by the classical soteriological models. If, then, we move up to that point of intersection, we may just be fortunate enough to jump the border, and get a sight of new vistas, previously denied to us. The image is not so fantastic as may at first appear, for if you consider how you set about introducing others to an experience you have had but they have not, you will find that your method is as above suggested. You search around to find the horizon of some experience they have had, which perchance intersects that which encompasses your special experience. When you find that segment of intersection, you next step is to lead them gently forward until they also stand at the point where the special subject of the search swims into vision. Maybe, in apologetics, that is the very arrangement which operates in reverse. You look for the segments of intersection of the traditional soteriological horizons with the areas of experience within which our contemporaries live and think; and having achieved that, we begin to build bridges across which traffic may move in both directions, so that *kerygma* may become communication, and the *skandala*, the stumbling-blocks to understanding themselves become stepping-stones to appreciation of the meaning of the death of Christ.

So much for the different ways in which we may try to explain and expound the inter-relations of the soteriological models to one another. Some may suit some tastes, some others. Some I find inadequate; others more picturesque and aesthetic, and useful in the short run didactically, but not quite strong enough to take heavy logical strain. It is the notion of dimensionality that most appeals to me, of those examined. But none is completely satisfactory or complete, for it is only ultimately in their relation to the single event which they individually seek to describe that they can properly then be related to one another. So, we turn to the second subject of this chapter: the relation of the models to the event of the death of Christ.

II.

At a first sighting, the question to which we now address ourselves, namely, the relation of the soteriological models to the death of Christ, looks very much like another question with which we are all too familiar in theology, the nature of religious language and of how it is possible for such language to describe the transcendent reality who is God. Admittedly there is some similarity between such an enquiry and the subject before us, and we shall certainly be invoking remarkably similar answers, nevertheless I should like to insist that ours are the rather different questions of asking what the implications are of describing the different soteriological models as 'models', and of how that description affects the question of the logic that governs them.

1. May I begin my answer to that question by drawing attention to the use of the term 'model', and by recalling Ian S.Barbour's discussion of 'theoretical models' (*Myths, Models and Paradigms,* SCM Press, London, 1974, p.30), which is the closest of his categorisation to our present purpose. Theoretical models are imaginative constructs, 'postulated by analogy with familiar ... processes, and used to construct a *theory* to correlate a set of *observations*... The model drawn from the familiar system suggests a theory...also possible relationships between some of the terms of the theory and some observation

terms'. The purpose of the model is the provision of a theory which yields an interpretative description of the nature of the observed events, and in so doing makes a tentative ontological claim and a tentative truth-claim. The relevance of this account of models to our question of the status of the soteriological models may be pursued in the following terms:

1.1 First of all, while it may seem somewhat extravagant to think of the soteriological models as 'imaginative constructs', the description will not appear altogether inept if we consider the way in which these models evolved. When the death of Jesus occurred, it was so far beyond the range of the experience of the disciples that there were no immediate categories at hand to enable them to comprehend it, let alone to communicate it. As the truth began to dawn on them, no doubt assisted if not primarily inspired by the Emmaus road conversation, they looked for, or were directed towards, images and ideas from their own experience and from Israel's faith that might be used to describe their Master's death. As the young church grew and taught its message to an ever-widening circle of listeners and disciples, new models were drawn upon to facilitate communication and to deepen understanding. The epithet 'imaginative' does no less than justice to the intuitive perception and selection of models, from the wide range of possibles, which were destined to mediate salvation to, and sustain the devotion of, century after century of Christian men and women.

1.2 Secondly, Barbour offers a clear account of the relation of the models to the theories, namely, that it is the role of the models to provide the theories. So, if we apply this account to our previous discussion of the soteriological models, we see that each model generates its appropriate theory. The use of the model, in the first instance, fosters the development of the details of the theory, but in doing so, integrates and co-ordinates such details. For example, the model of sacrifice becomes the centre of attraction for the many passages in the

Old Testament, which portray the cultus of Israel, and at the same time, is the medium of the association of them with the death of Christ, and of their transformation in their new application. In a later age, the model of satisfaction, drawn from the family-system of medieval society and its economy, supplies the values and the relationships which suggest structures and roles to be explored in the satisfaction theory as applied to the death of Christ. So the theory, in performing the functions just mentioned, incorporates within itself both the model and the objective event which it is endeavouring to describe. The theory is a statement which speaks about the death of Christ in terms of one or other of the models.

1.3 Thirdly, Barbour, in his account of models (particularly at p.32, *op.cit.*), draws attention to the importance of analogy for a proper understanding of their nature. So, in view of, and with the help of, the variations in accounts of the concept of analogy, we ought perhaps to look more closely at this general statement that there is analogy between the models and the subjects with which they are correlated. Two brief preliminary comments may be made. The first is that I should like to reserve my position on one aspect of that logic, namely, the case for the much criticised concept of the *analogia entis,* so widely rejected by Reformed theologians. It seems to me to be a firm obstacle to any proposal that the models are mental fictions or heuristic devices. But the second comment must immediately follow the first, as its justification: in parallel with the concept of the *analogia entis,* we should also find a place for its companion in controversy - the concept of *analogia fidei,* which contains the truth that it belongs to faith, inspired by the Spirit, to see the ordinary usages of language to be applicable analogically to what we say about the activities of God and his work in Christ.

Approaching now the detail of the relevance of traditional analogy theory to the question of the logical status of models, we may recall that, in our earlier discussions we designated the models to be incomplete symbols, which was intended at that stage as a fairly neutral term, and that error arose when the attempt was made, as it was by some theologians, to press the literality of the symbol, to treat it, that is, as a complete symbol. That would be the error of regarding the analogy, implicit in the models, as a form of generic predication, the use of the same term to describe a variety of entities belonging to the same genus. In other words, it would amount to saying that terms, such as, sacrifice, atonement, ransom, and so on, have precisely the same meaning when applied to the death of Christ as they have in everyday usage. Such a view has only to be stated to be rejected.

A second account of the nature of analogy may, however, prove more illuminating. For the models might interestingly enough constitute a case of analogy of proportion, or attribution. The example often given of this form of analogy is the application of the term, 'healthy' the so-called 'secondary analogate', to three different entities, namely, healthy food, healthy medicine and healthy complexion, all related, albeit differently, to the single healthy organism or person, which is the 'prime analogate'. Food maintains the health of the person; medicine restores his health; while a certain complexion is a sign of his health. Yet it is the same, single health of the person to which they are all so differently related, which justifies the application of the term 'healthy' to each of them, despite their great differences from one another. In much the same way, a ransom is said to be 'salvific', an act of penitence, a punishment, an act of reconciliation, a sacrifice, and an act of penal satisfaction, describable all in the same way as 'salvific'. These individual acts or events are not members of the same genus; but they do acquire the same single designation of 'salvific' through being related to the single act and event which is the saving death of Jesus Christ. Analogy of proportion was once

employed by Barth (*Church Dogmatics,* ET pp.267ff.) following Quenstedt who, according to Barth, had been unfaithful
to his Lutheran heritage; but it is usually replaced by Barthians
as by Barth himself on other occasions, by analogy of proportionality, which, I would have to say, might just be made to
apply in the present context. Remembering that analogy of
proportionality has the structure - a:b::c:d::e:f, or, a is to b as
c is to d as e is to f, and so on, we might say that the death of
Christ within the salvific purposes of God fulfils a role propor-
tionate to that fulfilled by sacrifice within the Jewish ritual
system; or the death of Christ makes good the honour of a holy
God who has been disobeyed by sinners, in a somewhat similar
way to that in which someone within the medieval feudal
system satisfies the overlord whose dignity has been offended
or whose interests have been damaged through some wrong
done to him by his subjects. The similarity or proportionality,
as it is more properly termed, may then be drawn between the
death of Christ and the other soteriological models.

So, what is emerging is that both analogy of proportion
and analogy of proportionality can be pressed into the
discussion of the logic of the models. For my own part, I have
found satisfaction in a somewhat simpler way of dealing with
the question, which incorporates most of what these classical
treatments have been presenting. It runs thus: if we say that
there is an analogy between sacrifice in the Jewish ritual of the
Old Testament (the *analogans*) and the death of Christ (the
analogatum), we would be intending that in respect of
characteristics A,B and C they are similar to one another, but
in respect of characteristics p,q and r in the *analogans*, and r,s,
and t in the *analogatum*, they are distinctly different from one
another. We would expect to find characteristics A,B and C
in each of the soteriological models we listed, as well as
characteristics in which they differed from one another and
from the death of Christ.

Two very important consequences follow from this way of presenting analogy. The first is that, through its application to the death of Christ, what began as an analogical application of a model becomes the primary significance of it. Professor Gunton, though he is speaking of soteriological 'metaphors' where we have been using the term 'models', (a subject to which we shall soon return) has this very point in mind when he writes, (*Op.cit.,*p.82), 'Metaphor, then, - when it is filled with meaning by gift of [the Holy] Spirit - expresses the truth of this matter, which is God present savingly to his world'. He had put the same point earlier in the book, (pp.50f.), asking 'May it not be that the theological use (of the soteriological metaphors) operates normatively and so alters the original meaning of the word in its everyday employment? In such a case, the new, metaphorical, meaning of the word would reflect light back on to the context from which the word was originally taken'.

The presence of those respects in which the *analogans* and the *analogatum* resemble, and differ from, one another has led to the drawing of a distinction which modern treatments of analogy favour, namely, that between the positive analogy and the negative analogy, the former being the elements in the two subjects of comparison which are similar and justify the comparison, the latter being the dissimilarities whose presence is necessary if we are to have analogy at all, rather than univocity. We did observe something not unlike these features of analogy when we referred to the soteriological models as incomplete symbols, because in each case so much of the symbol was applicable and valid, while the remainder was not. It is a distinction of great importance in all theology, but not least of all in soteriology, where, if we forget it, we begin to misrepresent the central event of the Christian faith. The presence of both the negative and the positive analogies is exactly what makes analogy, analogy, and distinguishes it from both univocity and equivocity, the former being the totally literal application of a term to two subject described by it, and the latter the totally ambiguous application of it to them. This distinction is for me so fundamental that I fail to follow Dr Janet Martin Soskice when (in *Metaphor and Religious Language,* OUP, London, 1985, pp.66) she says that 'Equivocation, univocation, and analogy are all types of literal speech and nowhere concerned with expanding descriptive powers'. What she says is obviously true of equivocation and univocation, but misrepresents the functioning of analogy, which can scarcely be regarded as a form of 'literal speech', as we have been trying to show, in discussing negative analogy.

1.4 Continuing with commentary upon Barbour's account of models and theories, (*vide supra,* pp. 67 f.), we now consider his view that the purpose of the model is the provision of a theory which makes an ontological claim and a truth-claim. He rejects such views of models as, for example, those which regard them naively as replicas of the structure and nature of the world or its parts, or those which take them to be ways of categorising experiences or observations, or valuable heuristic devices, which enable the investigator to learn more about his subject, but which have no capacity for genuine description of the way things are. He opts, on the contrary, for what he calls 'critical realism', which, while not committing itself entirely to the view that the models are totally representational, does believe that 'there are entities in the world something like those described in the model' (*Myths, Models and Paradigms,* p.42). Janet Martin Soskice was to echo that position, when she affirmed (*Metaphor and Religious Language,* p.123) that 'it is models and the web of metaphor which they give rise to which commonly constitute the means by which to speak of transcendent, but putatively real, entities and relations'. She had earlier (p.120) spoken of scientific explanations which depend upon models as reality depicting' and again (p.132) as providing 'epistemic access'. When, therefore, we employ the soteriological models of ransom, sacrifice, reconciliation, atonement, salvation and so on, in speaking of the death of Christ, we are not employing mental fictions on the truthfulness of whose reference we can not be other than agnostic; we are genuinely speaking of his death in these terms.

Janet Martin Soskice, however, qualifies her statement of the critical realist position, when she adds later (*op.cit.,* p.145) that 'models and metaphorical terms, may, in both the scientific and religious cases, be reality depicting, without pretending to be directly descriptive'; while Colin Gunton puts a similar view,(*op.cit.,* p.65),'These biblical metaphors .. are ways of describing realistically what can be described only in the indirect manner of this kind of [metaphorical] language. But an indirect description is still a description of what is really there'. The case that is being made by both writers is understandable, for they are rightly hesistant about any suggestion that human language can ever describe God as he is 'in and for himself', and that would, presumably, be comprehensive and veridical description, and direct in that sense. But allowing for a proper diffidence over making any such claim for religious language, I find some difficulty in combining the statements that the language of the 'models and metaphors' is, at the same time, realistic, indirect and descriptive of God and his activities. I would certainly wish to retain the term 'realistic' for the kind of description which the models and metaphors provide, for they depict genuine characters of their subjects, even though not comprehensively or infallibly. In other words, there is no implication either that such description provides a mirror-like representation of the world, and, in theology, of God and the person and work of Christ, or, on the other hand, that it expresses all aspects and relationships of those subjects to which it directs our attention, without any possibility of revision of its deliverances. My reluctance to use the word 'indirect' in this connection is that it leaves a gap between the models and the metaphors, on the one hand, and, on the other, those entities and relations, which they describe. If, however, there are misgivings over the use of the words 'indirect' and 'direct', perhaps there would be no loss in abandoning both. We could achieve the purpose of the two terms, if, in deference to the term 'direct', we recognised that the models and metaphors and the theories and the statements in which they are engrossed are descriptive of the real characters of their subjects, and not of mental attitudes or heuristic fictions; and, in deference to the term 'indirect', we acknowledge that we do not know and we can not describe these subjects other than in terms of the models and metaphors.

2. It is impossible, however, in any discussion of models, to avoid including with it an examination of metaphors. We have already found it so. Also, because of the immense popularity of metaphor in recent works on religious language, and notably, in the present field, that of Professor Colin E Gunton, *The Actuality of the Atonement, A Study of* Metaphor, Rationality and the Christian Tradition, T&T Clark, Edinburgh, 1988, I should like to place metaphor in relation to what has been said previously about models and theories. Above (at p.67), following a suggestion of Ian Barbour's, we observed that it is the role of the models to generate theories, in the case of soteriology, the models of ransom, sacrifice, reconciliation and so on, providing the well-known theories of the atonement. Such theories would take the form of statements, such as that 'The death of Christ is the ransom offered for the salvation of sinners'; or, 'The death of Christ is his self-sacrifice for sinners'; and similar theory-statements could be made out for each of the other models. The model, by constituting the underlying analogy for the theory, the analogue as it might be called, creates the conditions for the development of the theory. The means whereby the theory develops is the web of metaphors

(Soskice's phrase, *op.cit.*, p.123) which spin out from it, and give it articulation and extension. I would not like to appear, through these distinctions, unduly meticulous and hair-splitting. My purpose is to secure the fact that the model is not, or is not normally, a word or a sentence, but it receives its linguistic expression through incorporation in a theory or in metaphorical statements which expand the theory. On these grounds, I would have to resist Professor F.Ferré's suggestion (*Soundings* 2, 1968, p.334 Art. 'Metaphors, Models and Religion') that models are a kind of metaphor, for the reason that models and metaphors play distinct roles in the presentation of Christian doctrine. Those text-books which have traditionally expounded what they called 'the theories of the atonement' have been correct, in their awareness of what theological theory does. Where they fell short was at the next stage, when they failed to see how the theory expanded into the metaphors appropriate to the model on which the theory was drawn. This omission was serious, for not only did the metaphors help to expand the theory to its fulness, but they also helped to bring to light the full logical structure and status of the theories. Once we have determined the place of metaphors in the economy of theological, and therefore of soteriological expression, we may pay them closer attention. For example, if when we use models we are regarding one thing in terms of another, then, when using metaphors, we do the same sort of thing, but we do so explicitly and propositionally. Also, metaphors participate in the capacity of the models and the theories to be 'reality depicting', and to give cognitive access to the nature of the persons and the events that they describe. Metaphors, moreover, belong to the group of statements structured logically along analogical lines. But because in theology the subject or subjects to which they refer are God and Christ and their actions in the world, the reference may impart a normative quality to the metaphorical term, so that it becomes its true meaning.

Having thus given a place to metaphors within the analysis of the logical status of models, roughly in line with a number of contemporary works on the central part which metaphor is thought to play in religious linguistic usage, honesty compels me to acknowledge my uneasiness over the popularity which this kind of emphasis enjoys. What worries me is the very considerable difference between the ratio of negative to positive analogy in religious language and that ratio as it occurs in ordinary language. In the case of the metaphorical statement, 'The camel is the ship of the desert', the positive analogy would consist of the fact that both the ship and the camel are able to transport people across trackless wastes, which could well otherwise impede their travel. The negative analogy, on the other hand, would comprise, on the part of the ship, the possession of funnels, diesel engines, a rudder, and so on, and, on the part of the camel, the possession of a hump, a central nervous system, a knowledge of the secrets of Allah, and other such qualities. But clearly, the ratio of the negative to the positive analogies is high; so much so that the two subjects related to one another in the metaphor seem almost to differ in every other respect than that which forms the foundation of the metaphor. Indeed, the metaphor only 'works' when this is so. In the specific terms of the example we considered, the metaphorical statement, 'The camel is the ship of the desert', implies that a camel is *not* a ship. In other words, a high ratio of negative to positive analogy would appear to be constitutive of metaphorical statements appearing in ordinary communications, and there has to be a diminishing point beyond which the metaphor passes into literal statement. On the contrary, that ratio of negative to positive analogy seems to be reversed in religious statements categorised as metaphorical. The similarity, for example, between the death of Christ and ransom, the basic analogue obtaining between them, does not hold for one single point only, but, while there are differences which have not been denied, the basic analogue has generated a whole range of metaphors, which highlight the similarity. So, too, if we take the religious metaphorical statement, 'Jesus Christ gave his life a ransom for many', we see at once that we can not follow the logic of the earlier non-religious metaphorical statement, and say that this religious metaphorical statement implies that the death of Jesus is *not* a ransom. Indeed, had that implication held not only for ransom, but for all the other metaphors which appear in soteriology, this discipline would have been nullified from the start. But we reject the implication for a reason which has earlier emerged, namely, that when these different metaphors are employed in relation to the death of Christ, and so acquire a soteriological reference, then, as we have already quoted Colin Gunton as saying, (*vide supra,* p. 72), 'the theological use operates normatively and so alters the meaning of the word in its everyday employment'. The soteriological reference becomes the real and primary reference of these terms, and the everyday usage, not so much metaphorical in some dramatic reversal of roles, as deviant from the norm. What had begun as metaphor ends by being a statement about the nature of things and events, as they are.

Where do these non-popular reflections leave us? Total consistency might seem to suggest that we drop the use of the term 'metaphor' in connection with the analysis of soteriological language, leaving open the question of its relevance to general theological language. On the other hand, we might overlook what could be a fair discrepancy between religious and everyday use of metaphor, and recognise that metaphorical usage in soteriology develops into genuinely real and primary usage. With this qualification, and the acknowledgment that metaphor fits into the logic of model and theory as stated above, the discussion of the doctrine of the atonement is greatly assisted by pursuing the insights which they yield.

3. A form of this same 'negative analogy', I suspect, invalidates the application of another theory about religious

language which had great vogue for a number of years, due to the inspiration of Wittgenstein. It was the 'as' theory, the notion that religious statements can be reduced to a paradigm form, thus: 'I believe in the Fatherhood of God' transcribes as 'I see God as my Father'; or 'I believe in God the Creator' transcribes as 'I see God as the Creator'; the virtue of this way of reading religious stetements being thought to be that it relieves the religionists of the responsibility of actually stating that God is our Father, and so to be making claims that require to face verificationist challenges; or stating that God actually *created* the world, and so entering into competition with other views of the origin of the universe. But in addition to what thus amounts to a sell-out on the subject of ontology and fact, the 'as' theory falls foul of the 'negative factor'. As I have pointed out elsewhere, if I say, 'I see Charles as a brother', my statement only makes sense if Charles is not my brother. So we are going to make no progress in our analysis of the relations of the models to the death of Christ, if we employ the 'as' formula, popular as it still is in some quarters. It does not help our enquiry at all to be told that the church down the ages has seen the death of Christ as ransom, satisfaction, sacrifice, and so on, if it is implied either that there is suspension of judgment as to whether these terms really apply to his death, or that in fact his death was none of these things, but is only 'seen as' being so.

4. After referring to the biblical text on ransom, I might be thought to be obliged to consider another biblical form of expression, namely, the parable. A strong case can be made for regarding the parable as one of the major forms of Christian religious statement. The evidence is the way in which Jesus chose to give us the central elements of his teaching in parabolic form - concerning the love of God the Father for his children, the wealth of the provision that he makes for them, the forgivingness of the Father and the responsibility on all of us to forgive in a like manner, and so on; using for this

parabolic purpose the ordinary everyday things known with great familiarity by all his listeners. Now Jesus does employ a parable to describe his death, (Mt 21.33-46;Mk12.1-12;Lk20.9-19), the parable of the wicked husbandmen, which relates his death to the purpose of God. But we do not have an extensive run of parables in the New Testament to match the series of models we have before us in the history of soteriology, even though, as has been noted, they are almost all of biblical origin. So, while I should dearly have liked to be able to say that the models represent so many parables of the death of Christ, I have to admit that there is not the story back-up in the scriptures to justify that assessment.

5. There is, however, another way of defining the logical character of the models of soteriology, which with purpose has not so far appeared in our discussion, namely, that they are so many *interpretations* of the death of Christ or the meaning of the death of Christ. This designation I regard as the most comprehensive of all, including even analogy and metaphor, and I have omitted it because it is beset by pitfalls. For example, it is not always fully appreciated that interpretation is only one half of a situation, the other half of which is that which is interpreted, often called 'the given' or 'the data', less frequently called 'the facts', which almost by definition are thought to be uninterpreted. Already we have encountered two pitfalls: first, 'the facts' are not proper bed-fellows for the other two, for the facts, truth about what actually happened, or what is the case, all come at the end of the process of interpretation. In a loose way, the detective may ask at the beginning of a case, 'What, then, are the facts?' but he knows better than anyone that facts are just what he does not have; they come at the end of the case, after all his questioning and following up of clues as well as red herrings. 'The given' or 'the data' are far from uninterpreted; they are a tissue of given-ness and crypto-interpretation, and again the detective has a major task in separating out what was

actually given and what was already the subject of interpretation. The disciples on the way to Emmaus had already begun,
as had all their fellows, to interpret the events of the last days
of Jesus' life and of his death and resurrection, with the aid of
such insights as their previous faith had given them. That
interpretation had already become part of their experience as
they stood at the cross and as they saw him buried. Therefore,
when Jesus came to impart to them the correct interpretation
based upon the scriptures which he unfolded before them, he
was having to deal with a situation which already was confused
by crypto-interpretation. So, rarely, indeed if ever, do we have
a clear-cut beginning of uninterpreted given data, clearly
distinguishable from the subsequent interpretation imposed
upon it. These pitfalls, as I have been calling them are, not really
impediments to our using the designation 'interpretation' to
describe the models, so much as warnings to us that these are
not valid ways of employing the notion of 'interpretation'. On
the contrary, the interpretation approach to the models, I
believe, provides the most illuminating and comprehensive
understanding of them.

What I should like to propose, following in the footsteps of
our friendly detective aforementioned, is that what we call facts
are a combination of given and interpretation, both of which
become modified through their inter-action with one another.
There are, of course, some facts which are fairly simple, where
the given and the interpretation achieve a match speedily, and
where there is no room for any variant interpretations. Now
there are also events or actions, which by reason of their
internal complexity comprise a considerable range of interpretations. The death of Christ I would regard as an event of that
kind, with the models as the interpretations which form the
internal structure of the event. By their compresence within
the act or the event they are modified by the given which they
encounter there, the dying of the Eternal Son of God, and by

their inter-relations with one another. We have already seen something of both of these processes. The application of the idea of sacrifice to the death of Christ results in the transformation of the way the term is then used, with its implications that the victim is the One who is offering the sacrifice. Satisfaction is usually offered in response to the demand to make amends for a wrong done, but in Christ's death satisfaction is provided far in excess of the moral requirements made even of the God-man, satisfaction which produces merit for all his sinful sisters and brothers. Normally the offending one is expected to make reconciliation if peace is to be restored, but in the death of Christ 'God was reconciling the world to himself'. We have seen, also, how within the complex of given and interpretations the different interpretative models, as I shall now call them, do modify one another, sacrifice and reconciliation, example and atonement, redemption and propitiation, ransom and victory, all at one and the same time making their own emphasis, and also blending with the insights of the others.

For the description of the complexity formed by the given and the interpretative models in this way within the death of Christ I have chosen two terms which bring out the meaning farther. One is 'constellational richness', where there is recognised, on the one hand, the co-ordination of of the models within an actually existing group, and on the other hand, their active influence one upon another within the coherence of the system. If we were to extend that particular metaphor farther, we could add that there is within the constellation a Sun from which the individual members of the constellation derive their light, their power and their being within the constellation. I have also used the figure of 'nuclear profusion', again to convey the idea that the models reside within a nuclear system, the elements of which are in balance with one another, mutually influence and condition one another, and are all of them themselves sustained and defined by the core of the nucleus.

Once again the variety of the models is reflected in the use of the term 'profusion'.

Both of these descriptions are highly metaphorical, and I would be as sensitive as anyone to the limitations of the metaphors involved. If they are misleading, then they are also expendable. What is not expendable, and what I trust is not misleading, is the double point about given and interpretation, about the death of Christ and the models which have been used in developing theories of the atonement: first, negatively, inter-pretation is not to be regarded as an optional extra to be superimposed, or not, at will, when an event or an action is being described, as if it were theoretical and not factual; and secondly, positively, interpretation in the form of the soteriological mod-els - ransom, sacrifice, penitence, reconciliation, penitence, and so on - is ingredient in, and part of, the death of Christ which they describe. You might put it this way: they are all involved in, and part of, what happened when Jesus died, and they are not after-thoughts contributed by even the most devout of Chris-tians, reflecting upon Jesus' death. Paul Tillich often spoke of the way in which a symbol participates in the reality which it symbolises, and so are different from signs which, once we have found the reality to which they direct us, no longer have any purpose or being. In the same way the models of salvation share in the reality of that which they, in a very real sense, embody. Accordingly, that fact in which God so wondrously wrought our redemption was not simply the event observed to happen on calvary's hill, and describable in minimal terms as the demise of a criminal at the hands of the Roman soldiery and at the instigation of the Jewish hierarchy - an event subsequently made the subject of a variety of elaborate theories and interpretations. On the contrary, the fact which is the root and ground of our salvation is that multi-dimensional event, which is all the things we have been saying about it in the models. Anything less is an abstraction, and if proceeded with, becomes a falsification.

I first became aware of this way of treating data and interpretation in relation to facts in a different context, where it is perhaps more immediately obvious, namely, in relation to the Incarnation itself. We might think of the given as the fact that a baby was born in Bethlehem on a given date; and regard the interpretation which we find in Jo 1.14, 'The Word was made flesh and dwelt among us, full of grace and truth' as being an addition, a kind of epiphenomenon, to the original fact, and lacking in its status of factuality. In opposition to that view, I would prefer to say that the fact of which we are speaking is the combination of the simple historical datum of the birth of the baby and the Johannine interpretative expression of that event in its fulness of meaning, which will include all that the concept of the Logos implies, and extends eventually to the affirmations of the chalcedonian creed. Anything less than that affirmation is to that extent an abstraction from the richness and the profusion of the fact of the Incarnation. What I am sure we have had to battle against here is an ancient epistemological heritage bequaethed to us by John Locke, of the distinction between primary and secondary qualities, which assigned hard ontological status to the former, and regarded the latter as psychological addenda to reality, whose actual existence was always a subject of controversy. So it has always been difficult to defend the position that reality is rich in both primary and secondary qualities, and to excerpt either of them from their combined co-existence is to be dealing with an abstraction less than real.

In a word, then, I am contending that when we speak of the death of Christ, we speak of a fact which is rich in internal interpretation contained in the several soteriological models which have occupied our attention. Let me conclude by addressing myself to four questions which must invariably arise when the kind of position which I have been advocating is considered. The first is the question of error. Obviously, there have been many other interpretations of the death of Christ apart from those we have examined - some of them offered by the opponents of Christianity, but some of them also by those who have esteemed themselves to be Christians. Not all of these will be true; some we know are not true. But does the fact that they, too, are interpretations of Christ's death automatically make them ingredients in its reality, sharing its ontological status? The answer to that question has to be negative, and the negative rests on two criteria of truth. The one is the simple bibical criterion, that any candidate-interpretation has to be congruent with the biblical acounts of the death of Christ; for example, the proposal that Christ's death was only apparent, because he had been drugged, would not agree with the biblical narratives. But secondly, in extension of that biblical norm, it has to cohere with the models which we have discussed here, if it is going to find a place within what I was calling the 'constellation' or the 'nuclear profusion' - a straightforward case of the coherence criterion of truth.

The second question that arises is: do the series of models mentioned constitute a closed canon, a question sharpened in its relevance by the fact that we have not had credal (as distinct from confessional) definition of the orthodoxy of any given soteriological theories? A supplementary question would be: if a new soteriological model were to appear - such as might have evolved from the religious philosophy of Teilhard de Chardin - would it have the status only of epiphenomenon, and never achieve the ontological status of those of our canon? I would not wish to say that the canon is closed, any more than anyone could legitimately have tried to do so, say, in 300AD before Nicaea and Chalcedon. But to establish itself such a model would have, first of all, to meet the two criteria abovementioned; and, most importantly, as we shall argue in our final chapter, it will, like them, have to demonstrate its capacity to be a mediating agency of the forgiving grace of God in the crucified

Christ to men and women. When these points have been met, then it has to be said that this new model has been discovered to be, like the others, ingredient in the richness of the fact which is the death of Christ. It, too, is part of the profusion which is the redeeming grace of God in Christ the Saviour.

The third question to concern us is: how do the theory of the 'reality-depicting' qualities of metaphors upheld by Richard Boyd, and the critical realist account of them supported by Janet Martin Soskice and Colin Gunton connect with the view proposed above of the relations of data, interpretation and fact to one another? My answer would be that this latter view is a logical sequel to them, in that it attempts to deal with a problem which they appear to leave unmentioned. If it is the case that the metaphors are 'reality-depicting', or if they provide 'epistemic access' to the reality which they describe - even if 'indirectly' as the exponents of these theories insist - then there surely remains a question of how the different qualities of the subject thus described or known are considered to exist, or rather, to co-exist, within that subject. It is not satisfactory to be agnostic in the answer to that question, for such agnosticism would nullify the claim of *epistemic* access. What is known is a single subject, and its qualities have an integrity within it. The view which I have proposed is an attempt to spell out how this integrity occurs, and, combined with what has been said about the genuine possibility of error and revision, is the pursuit of critical realism to its logical conclusion.

The fourth question takes us back to what was said earlier (*vide supra*,p.28) about 'inclusive theology'. Previously a plea was made against any premature elimination of any of the models, certainly of any of those which appeared on our list, and the question is whether that earlier position can still be maintained. My firm conclusion would be that the case for the inclusion of all the models is, in fact, strengthened, and it is two-fold. First, it has become clear that in the constellational richness of the event which is the death of Christ not only do the different models find a home, but in doing so they modify and, at the same time, enrich one another. It is wrong, therefore, to exclude one of them simply by equating it with its everyday meaning, or with its meaning in some other religious culture. It has to be seen in its true home and in it proper place, in the soteriological event. Secondly, when we consider the history of the doctrine of the death of Christ, we realise that it would be foolhardy, because of what is thought to be some cultural unacceptability, to discard any of them. The models have many times demonstrated their continuing capacity to re-live for different generations as circumstances and conditions have altered.

4

UNIVERSALISERS, RELATERS AND CONTEMPORANISERS

Traditional accounts of the theories of the atonement seem to exhaust their purpose at the point which we have now reached in our discussions, namely, the presentation of the models and, less frequently, consideration of their logical relationship to one another and to the fact of the death of Christ. However, no matter how comprehensive such presentations have been and how meticulous the logical analysis, they still remain at best interpretations of an event that is past, you might almost say, marooned in the past and in the irrecoverable pastness of the past. Yet, there are events in the past which have the curious character of transcending that past and integrating themselves in the present. Examples of such events would be the signing of Magna Carta, Luther's stand at Wittenberg, the Declaration of American Independence, or the French Revolution, the influence of which can be traced at innumerable points in contemporary history, of which they might be said to be part. When, therefore, we claim for the death of Christ, as an historical event, that it transcends its pastness, to become part of many later occasions, right down to the present time, we are not making a special claim for it. What we are now specially interested in, however, is the way in which the Scriptures and the Church have understood this transcendence to be mediated and effected. The biblical media of such transcendence and effectiveness I call 'the soteriological prepositions'. They are as much part of what the Scriptures have to say about the death of Christ, and as determinative, especially through the conceptual adjectives which they generated, of the theories of the atonement, which the Church has constructed, as the models which are so often given pride of place.

The plan we shall follow is as follows: 1. to discuss in detail the soteriological prepositions, and the subtle variations among them; and 2. to expound their role in the understanding of the process of salvation; 3. to examine the effect of their conceptualisation, adjectivally, on the development of soteriology; and 4. to consider certain other media of the process of universalising, relating and contemporanising.

I.

THE PREPOSITIONS

1. We begin with ἀντί, *anti*, which may be variously translated as 'for' meaning 'instead of', in the case of the substitution of one thing for another, as Mt 5.38, 'an eye for an eye', or Lk 11.11, 'instead of a fish, a serpent', or 'for' meaning 'on behalf of', as Mt 17.27, 'give it to them for me and for yourself'. The classical occurrence of the preposition *anti* is Mk 10.45 = Mt 20.28, 'The Son of man came... to give his life a ransom for many'. In this text the preposition 'for' spells out as 'instead of', 'as substitute for', and even 'in exchange for' or 'in return for', the latter two also being normal translations of *anti*.

Let me make three comments on our first preposition: 1.1 It is already clear that there is a variation of meaning in the word *anti* which interestingly enough comes to light in the English translation, bearing out a conclusion reached in discussion of the models, that translation has often influenced soteriological theory. 1.2 We notice that the preposition is used sometimes with things (eye, fish) and sometimes with persons (many people), a circumstance in evidence in other prepositions. 1.3 The notion of substitution associated with 'for' meaning 'instead of' would seem to be a *hapax legomenon*, and only to have, therefore, the slenderest biblical foundation. The implied case against the use of this preposition in soteriological construction might be given some credence, were it not that the preposition occurs with the 'ransom' model, behind which lie, as I have argued in the chapter on the models, the Isaianic passages on the Suffering Servant, with their expiatory-sacrificial connotations central to the under-standing of Jesus' salvific role in Israel and among the nations.

2. Our second preposition is ὑπέρ, *hyper*, 'for' in the sense of 'on behalf of' which is, by far and away, the most frequently used of the soteriological prepositions. It occurs, for example, in St Paul's Epistles, at Rom 5.8, 14.15; I Cor 11.24,15.3; Gal 2.20; I Thess 5.10; and in St John's Gospel at 10.11, 10.15, 11.50f, 15.13, 18.14; also, at I Jo 3.16; Heb 2.9, 9.24, 10.12; I Pet 2.21; and most importantly, in Lk 22.19, 'This is my body which is given for you' and 22.20, 'my blood which is shed for you', both readings being omitted in some manu-scripts, yet having strong support in others. I find the full readings in these cases to be so consonant with the rest of the NT material on the meaning of the death of Christ and with the evidence of the liturgies, examined in chapter 1, as to be rendered virtually unassailable. Two comments are relevant:

2.1 Most of the nouns governed by the preposition *hyper* are persons, though, on at least two occasions, it is applied to things: I Cor 15.3, 'Christ died for our sins in accordance with the scriptures' where the meaning is almost 'on account of', and Heb 10.12, 'When Christ had offered.. a single sacrifice for sins'.

2.2 There is a subtle and interesting distinction between the form 'on behalf of' which we have so far been using *and* the form 'in behalf of', which appears in Robert Young's *Analytical Concordance to the Holy Bible,* Eighth Edition, Revised 1939, first published 1879, p.364, where it appears as the definitive translation of *hyper*, covering all the instances. At a first glance, it might be said that the 'in behalf of' is an archaism, and that 'on behalf of' is the modern and acceptable form of the phrase, were it not that a distnction can be drawn between them, which is still valid. 'In behalf of' means 'in the name of' or 'in the interests of', very much as a lawyer might be acting for his client, without the personal involvement implied by the phrase 'on behalf of', in the activity of someone who actually takes the part or the 'side' of another person for his benefit, or for his own sake.

3. The third preposition to engage our attention is περί, *peri*, which normally means 'concerning' or 'about', but drifts into meaning 'on account of' or 'for', when it is synonymous with ὑπέρ, *hyper*, for which it is not infrequently a textual variant. Its great claim to notice is that it appears in one or two very significant texts, such as, I Peter 3.18 and I Jo 2.2, but most importantly, in Mt 26.28, 'This is my blood of the covenant, which is poured out for many for the forgiveness of sins', and in I Jo 4.10, 'Herein is love ... that God sent his Son to be the propitiation for our sins'. There remain a number of texts where, in quite different connections, the preposition *peri* does not quite have its most general meaning of 'concerning' or 'about', but rather suggests the 'for' of the texts above mentioned, namely, Heb 10.18,26; Eph 6.11. Concerning *peri*, as used in the soteriological connection, we observe that its reference is to things (sins) and not to persons (sinners).

Having examined these three prepositions, we should observe in passing that there are two others, διά, *dia*, 'because of' and ἕνεκα, *heneka*, 'on account of' or 'because of', which have a meaning very similar to those we have just considered, which might have led to their employment in a soteriological connection, but in fact never do so occur.

Several points emerge from this rather detailed discussion of the soteriological prepositions and their Greek originals: first, there is no single established original Greek literary device used in the New Testament for the designation of the relation of the death of Christ either to sinners or their sins. Secondly, there are, on the contrary, three prepositions, which, when we pursue their English translations, yield variants of decreasing strength, taking 'instead of' or 'as substitute for' as the benchmark and proceeding through 'on behalf of', 'on account of', 'for' to 'in behalf of'. Thirdly, the fact that 'for' runs through the whole range leads to the conclusion that they are all in fairly close proximity to one another, and could even be said to merge into one another,which will prevent any fear that they might somehow be in contradiction to one another. Indeed, it would be possible to move in the opposite direction, and argue that they are all saying 'the same thing', but saying it with different emphases. Fourthly, the soteriological prepositions have been thought by theologians to be sufficiently distinguishable to create differing perceptions of the ways in which the death of Christ transcended the immediacy and particularity of an event which occurred in, say, 33AD, to embrace the sins of men and women in succeeding centuries of human history. In fact, it would not be out of place to use the phrase 'the prepositional dynamics' to refer to the forms of such transcendence which the prepositions generate. To them we now turn.

II.

The soteriological prepositions achieve this transcendence in three ways: first, as universalisers; next, as relaters; and finally, as contemporanisers. Let us deal with them in turn.

1. The very mention of universality in the context of soteriology at once calls to mind the long-running controversies over universal and limited atonement, which are endemic to the history of Presbyterianism. But there is, in fact, a prior question in soteriology relating to universality, namely, how it

is that an event, which took place so particularly in the first century, could be so universalised as to become available for men and women at every other time and in every other place in human history. It is a form of universalisation which makes possible both the traditional universalism and its theological opposite, limited atonement. However, to avoid that controversy for the present, because it has ignored, almost as if it did not exist, the logically prior question of the form of universalisation, which we are now considering, I have used, in my description of it, the phrase 'available for men and women' of later centuries; whether they all avail themselves of the atonement is the point at issue in the famous controversy. If we look more closely at texts already mentioned, familiarity with which has almost deadened our perception them, the role which the preposition plays becomes clear. 'The Son of Man came to give his life a ransom for many' (Mk 10.45 = Mt 20.28) or, 'God sent his Son to be a propitiation for our sins' (I Jo 4.10). If we look closely at the syntactical structure of each of these sentences, we see that the prepositional phrase with which they both end, the phrase introduced by one of the soteriological prepositions we were discussing, converts a statement about the past, 'The Son of man came to give his life a ransom', or 'God sent his Son to be a propitiation', into a statement with efficacy for mankind, with universal valency stretching well beyond the time of the past event.

A lot has been made of the concept of *Einmaligkeit* of Christ's redemptive death, by many continental theologians of this century, such as Brunner and Barth, in reaction, as already noted, against the Hegelianism of their early philosophical education. But it was also part of the witness of Reformed theologians anxious to deny any claims to the repetition of the sacrifice of Christ in the action of the Mass. No one would wish to deny the once-for-allness of Christ's death; as an historical event it was unrepeatable, *einmalig*. Yet one concern surely in the use of such language as 'sacrifice' and 'victim' in the Eucharist is that that once-for-all sacrifice and that Victim slain on Calvary should be so presented that redemption be made available and efficacious for the people of God. What I have been arguing is that the prepositional phrases, following as they do the historical statement concerning the death of Christ, are the media of the universalisation of that event, and secure the recognition of the universal availability of that salvation for all of human history. They do so, moreover, in a form which is acceptable to all denominations of the faith, and gives offence to none. In fact, they all incorporate it in some form in their doctrine and liturgy.

2. Secondly, the prepositional phrases act as relaters, which refer that once-for-all event, made available by the universaliser for men and women of every age and clime, to each and all of them. When St Paul wrote in I Cor 15.3, 'Christ died for our sins according to the scriptures', in using the phrase, 'for our sins', he was saying that the death of Christ was related to them and their sins, each one, in particular. It was as if they were each and all already, from the beginning, embraced within the salvation accomplished in the death of Christ. It was Melancthon - was it not? - who wrote *Christum cognoscere eius beneficia cognoscere*, 'to know Christ is to know his benefits', the benefits of salvation and all the power of his redeeming grace. Here, then, is what I have been calling the dynamic of the soteriological prepositions, which carries the original event of the death of Christ out beyond its setting in first century Israel, to earth itself in the sins and follies of men and women in other times and places, and to bring them offers of, and the reality of, forgiveness and renewal. So, when we speak of the death of Christ as an event which transcends history, we are thinking of a transcendence with a very special direction and purpose. The direction is towards the lives of individual men and women, and its purpose is their redemption.

3. Thirdly, the soteriological prepositions are contemporanisers, which, on the one hand, make men and women of today, or indeed, of any day, contemporaries of Jesus and of the cross on which he died then; and conversely, which make Jesus who lived and died then, a Saviour contemporary with them now. The historical gulf which separated all subsequent generations of Christians from the generation in which Christ lived was a problem which especially concerned Kierkegaard. It was so because of the scepticism which he adopted concerning the reliability of historical knowledge and which he injected into theological method for well over a century. He himself attempted to escape the consequences of isolating the disciple of today from the Saviour of yesterday, which would place the eternal happiness of the individual at risk, by proposing the 'Leap'. This Leap, what we would call the leap of faith, was calculated to overcome the ambiguities of historical knowledge by means of an existential decision which set the disciple of today in an immediate relationship with Christ and his benefits.

Without in any way wishing to diminish the importance of the place of faith in the process of salvation, I would like to question the analysis which motivated him to affirm the notion of the Leap, namely, his acceptance of the great gulf set between Christ's death then, and the availability of its benefits for us now, the gulf set by his historical scepticism. Actually, in a phrase which he invented, namely, 'the contemporary disciple', he gives us the solution to the problem which was in a sense of his own creating. It was a notion of which he was rather fond, and he devotes Chapter IV of *Philosophical Fragments* to the subject of 'The Case of the Contemporary Disciple', in which he writes, 'In [faith], every non-contemporary becomes a contemporary',(p.57) and the only disadvantage under which the non-contemporary labours is the creation over the intervening centuries of 'much gossip', 'foolish chatter' 'untrue and confusing'. Our argument is that that contemporaneity of the disciple with the Master and of the Master with the disciple is implicit in the use of the prepositions, when they add to the past fact that 'Jesus gave his life a ransom' the words 'for many'; or to the fact that 'Christ died, according to the scriptures' the reference 'for our sins'. The great gulf pictured by Kierkegaard as being totally divisive of Christ from those for whom he has died is a delusion, dispelled in that very act and event in which our salvation is accomplished. Consequently, we enter in to 'the benefits of Christ' not by seeking to go out from the present moment into an irrecoverable past, not even by the Leap, but rather through exploring the position in which we have been already set by Christ in his death, a position which is already bi-polar in that Christ has himself transcended the space and time between us, to make us his contemporaries.

It is, however, impossible to proceed in the present discussion without taking account of the present relevance to it of the doctrine of the Holy Spirit. As we have described the roles of the soteriological prepositions, the reader might be forgiven for thinking that the dynamic which we have attributed to them was competent of itself to effect the salvation of those for whom Christ died. Put briefly, the work of the Holy Spirit is to create the adequate response of men and women to the various forms which the transcendence of the death of Christ to the pastness of its occurrence takes. To elucidate the part which the doctrine plays in the subject of our study, we may avail ourselves of the objective/subjective distinction. We may say that the soteriological prepositions create 'the objective possibility' of salvation in fulfilling their three roles: objectively, they universalise in time and place the availability of the salvation effected in the death of Christ; they relate that death to the needs of each and all of God's creatures despite its universality; and they contemporanise the circumstances of that death as described by the several models with the disciples of every generation. But that objective possibility is only realised, and individual men and women appropriate the offer of salvation, when 'the subjective possibility' of salvation is present in the person of the Holy Spirit. He it is who creates the responsive decision of faith, which is the fulfilment of God's whole purpose in the death of Christ.

III.
CONCEPTUALISING THE PREPOSITIONS

It was claimed earlier that many accounts of the doctrine of the atonement exhaust themselves with the rehearsal of the theories developed from the models, to the neglect of the part which the soteriological prepositions play in the full development of the doctrine. Having considered both the variety of meanings of the prepositions themselves, and their roles in soteriology, we turn now to the ways in which these prepositions have been conceptualised adjectivally to provide further enrichment, some would even say, further controversy. These adjectival conceptualisations are: 'substitutionary', 'vicarious' and 'representative'.

1. The description of the death of Christ as 'substitutionary', associated with the word ἀντί, *anti*, 'instead of' or 'in place of', has a long-established place in the history of soteriology, but is not strongly supported scripturally if we confine ourselves to the New Testament (Mk 10.45 = Mt 20.28). This base is extended considerably and greatly consolidated, as we have seen, if the 'ransom' text is interpreted in the light of Is 52.13 - 53.12. When the full force of the substitutionary concept is retained to describe the death of Christ, then Christ is seen as suffering in our stead the penalty and punishment which should have been visited upon us for our disobedience towards God. So, though the primary role of the term is adjectival, and because it is necessary to the full employment of the 'punish-

ment' model, it very often occurs with a role reversal taking place, and it becomes the substantive, to give us what almost looks like another soteriological model, namely, 'penal substitution'. As was the case with the model of punishment, the concept of substitution sustained criticism, sometimes to the point of rejection, not just by such writers as J. McLeod Campbell (*The Nature of the Atonement*, MacMillan, London. 1st Ed. 1856; James Clarke & Co., London, 4th Ed. 1959), R.C. Moberly (*Atonement and Personality*, John Murray, London. 1901) , and H.A.Hodges (*The Pattern of Atonement*, SCM Press. 1954), so that it is all the more refreshing to find Professor Colin E. Gunton,(*The Actuality of Atonement*, T&T Clark, Edinburgh. 1989, p.165) making a stand: '.. we have to say that Jesus is our substitute because he does for us what we cannot do for ourselves. That includes undergoing the judgment of God, because were we to undergo it without him, it would mean our destruction'.

2. The second adjectival conceptualisation of the soteriological prepositions to occupy our attention is 'vicarious' which etymologically is synonymous with 'substitutionary', and in secular literature actually means sometimes 'in place of', 'representative of' and 'on behalf of', thus covering all three of our soteriological adjectives. In soteriology, however, in a strange way it has had a separate history of its own. We have already mentioned its important place in McLeod Campbell's presentation, where it was associated with penitence. But it was given a rather different liaison by N.Bushnell (*The Vicarious Sacrifice*, Alexander Strahan, London. 1866), who while recognising that the term 'carries always a face of substitution, indicating that one person comes in place of another, it does not mean simply that ... Christ becomes penally subject to our deserved penalties' (*op.cit.,* pp.4-7). Despite the closeness of meaning, then, there has grown up a tradition in soteriology, of thinkers to whom the idea of 'substitution' is anathema, but

who find the epithet 'vicarious' wholly acceptable. If we try to draw up a spectrum on which to plot these terms, relating it to the spectrum for the prepositions, and beginning with what has already been noted, that 'substitutionary' derives naturally from the Greek preposition ἀντί, *anti*, 'instead of'; I would have no hesitation in correlating 'vicarious' with the Greek ὑπέρ, *hyper*, 'on behalf of', remembering, from Bushnell, that *hyper* has a residuum of 'substitution' in it. But equally, *hyper* faces in the direction of our third adjectival conceptualisation, namely, 'representative' to which we shall next be turning. To sum up these possible correlations: *anti*, 'instead of' goes with 'substitutionary' and inclines a little towards 'vicarious'; *hyper*, 'on behalf of' goes primarily with 'vicarious' and as such has affinities with 'substitutionary', but when taken as '*in* behalf of', or 'in the interests of', or 'in the name of' must be correlated with 'representative'. That summing-up leaves out περί *peri*, which operates across the whole spectrum, from 'substitutionary' as in Mt 26.28, 'This is my blood of the covenant which is poured out *for many* for the forgiveness of sins', to 'for' meaning 'on account of'.

3. The distinction between 'substitutionary' and 'representative' is not immediately clear, but it could be drawn in terms of the degree of the involvement implied by the two terms. The person who acts as a substitute actually stands in the place that should be occupied by the one for whose sake the substitution is taking place. It is as if the substitute were that other person. The representative, on the contrary, keeps his own place, and the one he is representing keeps his, but the representative is empowered to act on behalf of the other person.

If I may be permitted a somewhat irreverent illustration: the game of soccer has no difficulty with the distinction which concerns us. The substitute - 'sub' in the language of the game - sits on the bench at the side of the pitch, often blue with the cold if the venue happens to be some where in Scotland, until one of the players on the field is injured. The 'sub' takes over and fulfils in the ongoing play the part which the injured man had already been playing. On the other hand, in the international games, the Scottish Football Association selects representatives who will wear the Scottish jersey, who will play in the name of the nation but certainly not instead of the nation. Such representatives will, on the day, also have 'subs' on the bench, who will take their place if they are injured. In other words, substitutes may also be representatives, and there is a message from this homely illustration for soteriology, namely, that having made the distinction we should not apply it rigorously to the point of making the two elements in it mutually exclusive.

The person who has made the greatest single concentrated effort in modern times to distinguish these two obviously closely related concepts from one another is Dorothée Sölle in *Christ the Representative* (ET, SCM Press, London. 1967). Complaining that the distinction is one which is fast disappearing from 'current linguistic usage' - Dr Sölle can not have been a soccer fan - she sets forth with determination to put the record straight (*op.cit.,* pp. 20ff.). 'To represent someone means to take responsibility for him temporarily', in the hope that the decisions taken will meet with approval from the person represented, but in recognition that he can not occupy the other person's place - an unwitting echo of Horace Bushnell on the same theme. By contrast, in substitution, 'what is replaced is treated as unavailable, useless or dead'. 'The replacement represents the other completely and unconditionally' and the other becomes a thing, inert and 'fixed once for all in its particularity'. With the antithesis thus inflexibly set, and given both an economico-political antipathy to individual replaceability and a socio-philosophical conviction about the ultimacy of the value of personal identity, she sets the scene for her soteriology: 'the individual man is irreplaceable *yet* representable' (*op.cit.,* p.50). Transferred to Christ, the term 'representative' denotes that he is the summing up of humanity, and is our representative before God. Because he is representative, his action and his suffering are also represcentative, and applicable to all whom he represents, that is, to all mankind - the universalisation process, of which Sölle is also well aware, being very much in evidence. When, however, she rounds off this part of her case, she makes a statement (at p.69, *op.cit.,*) which goes beyond her initial description of representative, and somewhat throws her carefully drawn distinctions into confusion. 'The Representative assumes the identity of those he represents, the destiny of dying after meaningless life. He dies "for" them, that is to say, in their place. The "just" dies "for" the unjust'. The examples given previously (p.20) had ruled out this very possibility of the Representative taking the place of the person represented. On p.70, Sölle returns to this theme, holding that the representation of which she is speaking is 'an act of identification' in which 'Christ took our place voluntarily'. 'Identification' is a concept which is yet to concern us, and my own conviction is that it lies at the foundation of the whole discussion of substitution and representation; but its mention at this point in her account takes Sölle much farther in the direction of validating substitution than her previously stated views would logically allow her to go. Sölle does eventually violate her own distinction between substitution and representation, when (at p.70) she says that 'it is a vital element in Christ's existence as a person that his representation should be an unfinished and continuing relationship'. This statement does not accord with her previous claim that the representative plays only a temporary role when occupying the place of the person represented. In fact, the obstacle in the way of Sölle's using the notion of substitution to supplement the ideas she gathers under the heading of representation is her insistence that what is replaced in substitution is not only treated as dead; it is dead. This insistence arises from some deep psychological aggression against the very idea of substitution, which might have been produced by a previous hurtful experience. I do not know, but that single cirumstance has had a disturbing effect upon what is otherwise a very perceptive analysis of two central soteriological notions.

This distortion prevents her from seeing the strength of Barth's position (*Church Dogmatics,* IV/1, ET, pp.157ff) when he says, for example, that Christ 'has taken the place of us men ... in order (there) to act in our name and therefore validly and effectively for us ... representing us without any co-operation on our part' (*op.cit.,* p.230). Not only is Barth said to confuse substitution and representation, but consequently, according to Sölle, he also de-personalises the relationship between Christ our Representative and ourselves. So far is Barth from failing to distinguish between substitution and representation, that he is in fact implying that they merge into one another, reflecting something of the way in which the prepositions, as we saw, fell along a spectrum in which meanings shade into one another. Moreover, in taking exception to Barth's denial of any co-operation between ourselves and our Representative, which she feels de-personalises the relationship between him and ourselves, Sölle seems to be advocating a synergism of a strange kind. How could there be co-operation between sinners and their Saviour, at the point of his electing to be their Representative? Co-operation, if we may so name it, surely comes at the later stage, when the Holy Spirit leads men and women to receive the benefits of the forgiveness achieved in Christ's death, though even there 'participation' in the benefits of Christ would be a more appropriate way of describing the relation of redeemed sinners to Christ than 'co-operation'.

IV.
FURTHER MEDIA OF UNIVERSALISATION, RELATION AND CONTEMPORANISATION

So far we have been considering how the soteriological prepositions and the adjectives which they generated have been effective in universalising and contemporanising the once-for-all event of the death of Christ, so that it became the medium for the divine salvation of mankind. They so related that death to sinful men and women of all time, that they participated truly in the benefits of Christ. But in the history of soteriology the process which the prepositions inaugurated has been thought to be sustained in three further ways, in what we might call 'the soteriological operational substantives'. They are: imputation, recapitulation and identification.

1. The operation of *imputation*, which played so considerable a part in the thought of Calvin and Luther on the atonement, and even more perhaps in that of their successors, may be thought of as occurring at two points in the working out of human salvation. The first takes place when God does not impute to the sinner his sin, but instead imputes it to Christ, who can be imagined as saying, 'I did the sin which Martin did'. The second point of imputation arises when Christ has, as a consequence of the first imputation, borne the judgment of God against that sin, enduring the penalty which is just, deserved and necessary, and thereupon the merciful God imputes to the sinner the righteousness of Christ, exhibited in both his active and passive obedience. In some theologies this process is called 'the great exchange', for our sin and Christ's righteousness are exchanged for one another, to the salvation of mankind.

Scottish calvinism in its popular forms, when combined with a doctrine of double predestination, has failed to treat imputation in a satisfactory way. The classical expression of this unsatisfactoriness is to be found in Robert Burns' poem

'Holy Willie's Prayer'. In it, Holy Willie, because of his self-convinced membership of the elect, made no attempt to conceal his lecherous activities, and appeared to sense no incongruity between such behaviour and the righteousness which might rightly be expected of one who claimed to be redeemed of Christ. In short, imputation stands in constant danger of creating an unbridgeable gulf between imputed righteousness and genuine moral integrity.

Sölle, *Christ our Representative,* pp.75-77, attempts to redress the balance in favour of imputation against the criticisms of the last paragraph, very much in a post-calvinistic and post-lutheran mood, in two ways. First, she maintains that when God imputes righteousness to men and women, and regards them as righteous, there is no pretence in this act. In fact the imputation is 'a creative word which calls into being that which does not exist,' namely, 'the possibility of being righteous'. She rightly rejects the phrase that Melancthon employed to explain, and maybe as he thought to exculpate, Luther, *peccator in re, iustus in spe,* 'actually a sinner, but hopeful of being righteous', for it leaves the sinful nature of the sinner actually untouched by the redemptive power of Christ. Secondly, she argues that the notion of imputation is calculated to safeguard the truth that men and women do not possess righteousness in their own right, but only through their dependence upon God. These are two points well-made. II Cor 5.17 says quite clearly: 'If any man is in Christ, he is a new creation'. Certainly that new creation will be sustained in the new relationship with Christ. But the righteousness which characterises the life of that new creation in Christ is effective righteousness. It is not just *in spe;* it is *in re.* No one could be in Christ and live the life of Holy Willie.

2. Mention of the notion of life *en Christo,* 'if anyone is in Christ ..', leads naturally to a form of the universalisation principle, which, though it has had a wide currency in

Christology, has emerged as of major importance also in soteriology. It does not emanate immediately from the soteriological prepositions, but like them is a most significant expression of the manner in which the death of Christ transcends the historical particularity of its occurrence. The idea so economically and tellingly contained in the short phrase, *en Christo,* is that the redeemed Christian lives his/her life within what we now call the ambience of Christ. But this incorporation here-and-now is to be traced back first of all to the incarnation itself, when Christ assumed our humanity. Some theologians have argued that the humanity which Christ took was not the perfect humanity which God created, but humanity, soiled and defiled by human sin. So the patristic saying which gathers up this thinking, namely, 'what Christ did not take, he did not redeem' has had three implications for soteriology. First, from it the conclusion has been drawn that if Christ had not taken sinful human nature, then sinful human beings like ourselves would never have been redeemed. This position has understandably attracted much opposition, insofar as it seemed to be declaring Christ a sinner, and the support for the opposition has been the more influential in the history of Christology. Secondly, the saying has been converted from the negative to the affirmative, to give the statement, 'what Christ took, he redeemed'; and this form has in popular writing been regarded as summing up the Eastern Church's theology of redemption, namely, that redemption is effected through incarnation. Thirdly and consequently, when Christ dies upon the cross for the sins of sinful mankind, then, as St Paul says at II Cor 5.14, 'one has died for all, therefore all have died'. Because of their incorporation in Christ, sinful humanity having been assumed by Christ participate in his triumph over sin, as it were, from within the redemptive event itself. When the redeemed life goes on to express itself in day-to-day existence, it is lived *en Christo.*

When the redemptive purpose of God is conceived of as extending beyond human destiny, into the whole of history, of nature and the universe - a view of redemption of which we have been hearing a great deal from Christian ecologists, then the universaliser is not so much incorporation as 'recapitulation', *anakephalaiosis*, a notion which may be derived again from a *hapax legomenon,* Eph 1.10, where it is said that it is God's good pleasure 'to gather all things in Christ (who is their head), things both in heaven and on earth'. The theme is that God had a purpose for the whole of his creation, which was frustrated by the sin of man, who is regarded as acting in a representative capacity and brought the whole of creation under the judgment of God. So God gathered up the entirety of the universe, nature as well as man, in the single redemptive act of the death of Christ, and the benefits of that redemption were deployed cosmically into the whole of God's universe, and God's purpose for the whole of creaion was consummated.

I said earlier that this form of the universalisation principle is certainly not *prima facie* derivative from the prepositions which have been exercising us. Yet I wonder. For example, if we take a text such as I Cor 15.3, 'Christ died for our sins', we recognise at once that one major element in the possibility of the death of Christ transcending the particularity of all historical occurrence must surely reside in the character, the Person, as Christology would say, of Jesus Christ. The presence in the God-man who is the Redeemer, of human nature, which is itself of universal significance, is the guarantee of the universal availability of the redemption. Further, because this humanity of Christ's gathers up all humanity, his death is immediately referrable to men and women of all times and place, as it is immediately contemporary with them all. The point has been enshrined for us in the spiritual, 'Were you there when they crucified my Lord?' Answer: all humanity was there.

3. There is a third concept which operates as a universaliser and a contemporaniser; and which, I would claim, lies at the basis of most of our thinking about how we are related to Christ's death, and how he was related to us in our sinfulness. It performs the three-fold function of unifying the others, of controlling them, and finally of providing us with a category of great relevance to theological as well as pastoral thinking. The biblical origin of the concept lies in II Cor 5.21, 'For God hath made him to be sin for us, who knew no sin, that we might be made the righteousness of God in him'. The Sinless One in that quite unique act of self-transcendence passes over from being on one side, to identify himself with the wholly other, the unloving and the ungodly, who are the negation of his love and his righteousness. The identification was in evidence at the beginning and the end of Christ's public ministry upon earth. At his baptism, the Beloved Son, the Elect of God, received the baptism of John which was a baptism upon confession of sins and genuine repentance. Theology has always found that situation difficult of explanation, the difficulty being summed up in St Matthew's form of John's question to Jesus, (3.14), 'I have need to be baptised of thee, and comest thou to me?' Yet it was the identification of Jesus with sinners at their point of confession which was of the essence of his presence upon earth. The writer to the Hebrews (13.12f) put the complementary point in graphic way: 'Jesus also, that he might sanctify the people with his own blood, suffered outside the gate'. In other words, in his death also, as in his baptism, Jesus identified himself with the criminals, the rejects, all sinners at the point of their utmost dereliction and distance from God. He bore their griefs; he carried their sorrows; he descended into hell. The single concept to describe, and to extend the full meaning, of these situations is 'identification'. It was an emphasis which was heard in J. McLeod Campbell (*op.cit.* pp.137ff): Jesus Christ 'through the assumption of the identification of himself

with those whom he came to save, rendered the confession of our sins before the Father, and experienced an equivalent sorrow and confession'. Here 'identification' is the foundation of 'vicarious penitence'. Similarly in H. Bushnell (*op.cit.*p.7): 'Christ in what is called his vicarious sacrifice, simply engages, at the expense of great suffering and even of death itself, to bring us out of our sins and so of our penalties; being himself profoundly identified with us in our fallen state, and burdened in feeling with our evils ... Love is a principle essentially vicarious in its nature, identifying the subject with others, so far as to suffer their adversities and pains, and taking on itself the burden of their evils'. This time 'identification' is the underpinning of 'vicarious sacrifice'. Next, we come to H.R.Mackintosh, (*The Christian Experience of Forgiveness*, London, 1927. pp.118f): 'The language of imputation, if not displaced by identification, is interpreted by it'. Finally, James Denney, who employs the language both of 'reconciliation' and 'penalty' in his writing on the death of Christ, nevertheless balances the matter evenly when he sums up the impact of what Christ has done for us upon what our response to him should be. He describes it as that 'response of an indivisible faith in [Christ] in which we identify ourselves with him, as he has identified himself with us'. Once again 'identification', the identification of Christ with all his brothers and sisters in life and in death, becomes the basis upon which the whole atonement rests.

5

THE NATURE OF FORGIVENESS

I.

In the foregoing examination of the models and their appropriate logic, of the soteriological prepositions and their
adjectival conceptualisations, and of the other media which
relate the past event of the death of Christ to men and women
today, it will not have gone unnoticed that the word 'forgiveness' has appeared but rarely. So, despite the contemporanisers,
the relaters and the universalisers, all of which, as we saw, had
the plain intention of 'earthing' the different ingredients of the
once-for-all event of the crucifixion in the lives and hearts of
generations then unborn, there has remained a hiatus. The
actual consequences for these generations has not been spelt
out in the terms of forgiveness, as distinct from the modular
concepts which formed the nuclei of the theories of the
atonement, which made such forgiveness possible . It is as if we
had to extend St Anselm's classical statement to read, 'To this
end was he made man that he might die - and that men and
women through that death, might receive forgiveness'. This
chapter, therefore, could well be sub-titled 'atonement and
forgiveness', for our purpose now is to try to sketch the
relationship between the two. Nor could there be any more
fitting manner in which to round off that previous examination, for it is the whole design of atonement, as has just been
said, that men and women should come to know and be
renewed by, the redeeming love of God in Jesus Christ

109

crucified, through which they receive forgiveness for their sins against that same God and against one another.

Before we embark upon such a project, however, it will be necessary to consider two almost opposed objections to what we are proposing to do. The first of these comes to us with a very long history of support, clearly documented in St Anselm, *Cur Deus-homo,* where the indefatigable Boso as early as chapter six of Book One, charges Anselmus with the words, 'If God is willing to save the human race only in the way you [Anselmus] describe, when he could have done it by sheer will, to put it mildly, you disparage God's wisdom'. Here we have farther evidence, if we needed it, for the claim that in that work St Anselm anticipated most of the objections to a classical soteriology that have arisen in the history of theology, not least in the modern or modernistic expression of it in Paul Wernle (quoted in D.M. Baillie, *God Was In Christ,* London, 1947, p.172), 'How miserably all those finely constructed theories of sacrifice and vicarious atonement crumble to pieces before this faith in the love of God the Father, who so gladly pardons! The one parable of the Prodigal Son wipes them all off the slate'. There is not one of us who has not at some time or other either entertained this objection ourselves or had to try to answer it when charged to do so by a latter-day Boso.

Donald Baillie, in the work referred to, treats this objection so seriously that, in fact he offers, what amount to two attempts to answer it, both of them rather original. The first (at *op.cit.,* p.173ff) traces 'a faint analogy' to God's re-action to human sin in sorrow, love and forgiveness 'in the love of a true friend who receives a grave wrong but who generously forgives'. Such a friend will not pass over lightly or nonchalantly the sin committed or the hurt done to him. Caring deeply for me, he will experience my shame over the wrong more deeply than I do, and will suffer more than I do, not in a mood of self-pity, but because of the quality of his love. His forgiveness will, then, be no cheap or easy condoning of the offence, but will rather emerge from a profound anguish borne of love. This analogy has to be extended *eminentiori*, for as God's love far exceeds that of my friend, so will his forgiveness be drawn from an even deeper anguish and suffering. It is for me just a little strange that Baillie does not go on at that point to connect the anguish which God thus feels, to the crucifixion of Christ on the cross. On the contrary, he rounds off this very illuminating analogy with the reflection which omits actual reference to the death of Christ, that 'There is an atonement, an expiation, in the heart of God Himself, and out of this comes forgiveness of sins' (*id.*, p.175).Yet that death of Christ on the cross, the infinite suffering of the Eternal Son, in which the Father shares, is the measure both of that love and the anguish from which God's forgiveness emerges. Therefore, just because Baillie has not connected that anguish of God's over our sin, to the point of identifying it with the suffering of Christ; because, too, he has internalised it 'in the heart of God Himself', and not external-ised it in the history of crucifixion; I do wonder whether he has really answered the questions of Boso and Wernle and the countless others who wished to know why forgiveness should be associated with the death of Christ. As stated by Baillie, this anguish of God over our sin could be experienced by God in a most profound way, in his own heart, without issuing in the overt events of Christ's death. It may be that the analogy of my friend's sorrow over my offence against him is not sufficiently extensive to meet the case.

Baillie's second attempt to meet the problem of the relation of atonement to forgiveness follows the first. It is presented as an interpretation of the place which atonement, expiation, propitiation and reconciliation hold in the biblical theology of sacrifice in relation to human sin. The initial role of sin-offerings and guilt-offerings was to wipe out the ceremonial and ritual offences, and not the great moral sins, such as,

violation of the Decalogue, for remission of which no allow-
ance was made. In their case, an approach might be made to
God for mercy, but the normal expectation would be for
punishment. With the prophetic movement in the eighth
century B.C., two developments occurred. The prophets
declared first of all that what really offended God were the
moral evils of injustice, cruelty, violence, oppression of the
poor; and all the sacrifices in the world would be unacceptable
to God so long as these evils continued. The second declaration
of the prophets was that God *will* forgive these heinous sins,
provided the sinners repent their wrong-doing, amend their
ways and return to God. Given two such revolutionary decla-
rations, it might have been confidently expected that they had
sounded the death-knell for the whole sacrificial approach to
forgiveness. On the contrary. In the Post-Exilic period not
only did the sacrificial system increase in scale, but it now
extended to cover all the wrong-doing of the people, whether
ceremonial or moral. Explanations abound for why it was so;
but one serious possibility was the profound awareness that
such repentance as human sin required was beyond human
capacity, and repentance had still to be supplemented by
sacrificial offerings. With the advent of Christ, 'this extraordi-
nary climax' occurred, namely, on the one hand, not only is the
offer of forgiveness to the repentant sinner renewed, but also
where the sinner has not repented, God goes out himself to
seek the wanderer; and on the other hand, the comprehensive
vocabulary employed in the Old Testament within the
sacrificial system over several centuries - sacrifice, offering,
expiation, propitiation, and reconciliation - is now applied to
the interpretation of the death of Christ - but with certain
qualifications which we have previously ourselves observed.
God himself provides the sacrifice, and his Son is the victim.
'The victim and the priest are one' (*op.cit.,* p.178). God freely
and abundantly graciously pardons the sinner, but it is forgive-

ness which is infinitely costly. So free forgiveness and costly forgiveness are woven into one pattern in the New Testament account of the death of Christ.

My own judgment is that this second answer from Baillie to the question why God could not simply will the forgiveness of sinners without the intervention of the cross of Jesus, makes good the unfinished quality of his first answer in terms of the analogy from human friendship; though I can not say whether he so meant them to be combined.

Without intending to detract in any way from Baillie's answers, I would like now to look at two other possible responses. First, if we think of God's loving willingness to forgive the sinner, expressed in the call to repentance of the Prophets, as distinct from human understanding of that call and from human ability to make adequate response to it, we have to say that that love already encompasses the sacrificial cost of the cross. It would be little short of blasphemy to say that that love was deficient or in any way inadequate to meet any sinner's plea for forgiveness in Old Testament times, because the crucifixion had not yet taken place. In other words, there was no time when God's offer of forgiveness, or the implementation of that offer, was not made out of a love which had already embraced the cross. Two considerations may serve to enforce this response to our problem. In Revelation 13.8 there occurs a fairly obscure text which in the RSV reads, 'And all who dwell on earth shall worship it [the beast, of v.5], everyone whose name has not been written before the foundation of the world in the book of life of the Lamb that was slain'; but which in the KJV had read, 'And all that dwell upon the earth shall worship him [the beast], whose names are not written in the book of life of the Lamb slain from the foundation of the world'. I find it odd that the RSV should associate the phrase 'before the foundation of the world' with the clause 'everyone whose name has not been written', when, in, fact in the Greek original the phrase in question, ἀπὸ καταβολῆς κόσμου (*apo kataboles kosmou*) is separated from γέγραπται (*gegraptai*, written) by several phrases. Besides, 'before' is not a very apt translation of *apo* (from). So, once again fearing that theological considerations have been allowed to distort what is otherwise a straightforward text, I find myself adhering to the KJV phrase of 'the Lamb slain before the foundation of the world', and to the notion implicit in it that the suffering and the anguish of the cross were foundational elements in those attributes of God which we designate love and mercy. Consequently, when God is presented in the Old Testament as forgiving, he does so in virtue of a sacrificial love which is already endemic to his nature, even though it still has to be overtly fulfilled in the life, death and resurrection of Jesus Christ. This consideration is also basic to a theological tenet which has not always won great popularity, because it was embodied in the rather off-putting doctrine of supralapsarianism, that the decree of election holds precedence over the decree of creation, because God's will to make known his essential nature as a God whose mercy and forgiveness are rooted in sacrificial love is the foundation of his whole relationship to the created order of mankind and nature. So when God acts within that created order, he acts as the God whose love is both costly and forgiving - love, cost and forgiveness which reach their climax in the life, death and resurrection of Jesus Christ. Sometimes this point is made in other ways, in the contentions that the redemptive power of the death of Christ is retro-active to the previous history of Israel, or beyond it to people of other societies and cultures who have never come within the range of Judaism or Christianity; or that God offers forgiveness under the old dispensation, or even outwith it, *proleptically*, in anticipation of that forthcoming fulfilment of the sacrifice, through which his redemptive purpose is to be effected. The sophistication of these proposals should not obscure from us their intention, which is that wherever and whenever God offers to men and women his forgiveness, whether in Nineveh or Bashan, or at a well in Samaria or from a cross on Calvary, that forgiveness springs from love which is intrinsically sacrificial and costly. At no point, say, in the previous history of Israel, could he be conceived of as forgiving other than at the cost of that cross.

Of course, it might be possible to contemplate what A.E.Taylor used to call 'a short way' - a kindly philosopher's short shrift - with the the question we are considering, that of why it was necessary for Christ to die, that our sins might be forgiven, or why God could not simply and freely will to forgive our sins. Standing as we do on this side of Calvary, we receive a forgiveness which comes to us as an integral whole, forgiveness which is both freely offered to us, and which is costly to God, the two strands of which Baillie was speaking, woven indissolubly into one. To ask now whether it is possible to have one of these strands at the exclusion of the other is to ask an improper question. And further, such has been the nature of forgiveness throughout the whole of human history, even though it may have been only one strand that was visible or audible.

II.

Our purpose in this chapter is to delineate the relationship between atonement and forgiveness, and we have just been considering one very much publicised objection. We turn now to a second, which comes from a very different angle. It is the criticism that so comprehensive and complete are the so-called theories of the atonement, so thoroughly do they demonstrate how amply have God's requirements of sinful mankind to make amends for their rebellion against God been met by Jesus on calvary; that they leave the impression that there is in fact nothing remaining to be forgiven. I think that I would give two answers to this rather unexpected suggestion. The first is that it only seems to work because the word 'forgive' is being used in the sense which we rejected in our last section, namely, freely cancelling and condoning. What the objector has in mind is that while the main weight of reconciliation is carried by the atoning work of Christ, there has to remain a residuum of unforgiven sin which God graciously condones. We have already given reasons for rejecting such a concept, and we need not delay over it. Secondly, and more importantly, what this unacceptable suggestion fails to see is that these theories of the atonement are in fact descriptions of how forgiveness *works*. Of course, there is no residuum of unforgiven sin, because the whole of human sinning has fallen within God's conspectus in initiating, sustaining and accomplishing the work of salvation in Christ in the terms which we have been describing. But what our notional objector is trying to say is something much more important than we have taken account of in our two replies to his objection. It is that the different processes described in the various theories of atonement or redemption are not completed until actual men and women receive forgiveness from God through Christ for their sins. So we turn now to the question of the relation of atonement to forgiveness.

III.

What we are now embarked upon is the examination of the ways in which we have been considering soteriology to be shaped, the varying components which co-operate to give it its structure, actually eventuate in ordinary folks reaping the benefits of the work of Christ. Put more finely, what we are concerned with now is the content of the *est*, the 'is', in Melancthon's words *Christum cognoscere est eius beneficia cognoscere,* 'to know Christ is to know his benefits'.

1. The very first affirmation to be made is that the different theories of the atonement are so many accounts of the foundation upon which the forgiveness of his people by God rests, a

truth observed in the second of the objections discussed above, but employed there as a premise to yield wrong deductions. But the truth even though wrongly used was still a truth, and the major affirmation in all soteriology. For it is the statement of God's grace towards sinners, and since it ante-dates the human response to God's approach, and any possible human repentance, it is rightly called 'prevenient grace'. Therefore, the condition of every offer of forgiveness must be the telling and the hearing of the way in which God has laid the basis for such forgiveness. To that end I would want to counsel the telling of the atonement story and the variety of ways in which it has been understood and interpreted, in all their fulness so that nothing would be missed. Referring back to the notion of the event of the death of Christas comprising a whole range of ingredients represented by the different interpretations deployed from the models, we are saying that they all have their place in this complex foundation upon which human redemption rests.

2. One of the reasons for emphasising the importance of having all of the ingredients of the nuclear event which is the death of Christ presented in the description of the foundation and possibility of all forgiveness, is that the different models, in addition to being components in the event, also lay out the paths which men and women are to follow to find their way to that forgiveness. We have already drawn attention to the way in which in a slave society, the ransom model is already making contact with the depressed condition of the hearers; and even when the model is extrapolated to include not just economic circumstances but also spiritual, in human terms the understanding both of the meaning and the relevance of the death of Christ has already begun. In a culture in which a high value is placed upon personal relationships, the model of reconciliation must provide immediate intellectual and emotional inroads into how the death of Christ is to be understood and

appropriated. A generation which has come to interpret its spiritual condition in terms of guilt - for the poverty of the so-called proletarian class, if the charge is made against a capitalist society by a marxist critic; for the condition of the Third World, if the charge comes from an anti-imperialist anxious to lay the blame for its hunger and under-development at the door of the West; for the state of the environment, if the ecologist has anti-Calvinist tendencies and is attacking the Presbyterian establishment - a generation, I say, processed, programmed, you might add, to think of its culpability for these and other situations, might well turn to a soteriology strong in talk about expiation and atonement. There might well arise other situations where the appropriate soteriological model would 'chime in' with the equivalent spiritual distress of the hearer.

The following comments might be here in place. First, while it is true as a generalisation that it is sin which is forgiven through the atoning death of Christ, and, as we shall later be considering, it is fellowship with the forgiving and loving God which is thereby achieved; nevertheless, that sin - how shall I put it? - makes itself felt in a variety of different ways, to which the different models answer. St Paul, in a classic statement, said the ' the wages of sin is death' (Rom 6.23), and in extension of that idea, we may make our point in either of two ways. On the one hand, we may say that this death which is the wages of sin may take the many forms adumbrated by the soteriological models, of bondage to habit, desires, or whatever is our enslavement; of alienation, defeat or guilt; or whatever it is that separates us from God and produces spiritual emptiness or rebellion. On the other hand, we may say directly, and without the inter-position of the reference to 'death', that the wages of sin is one or other of these conditions I have just mentioned. Either way, this breaking down of the notion of sin has the advantage of furthering the process of self-analysis and of self-awareness, which is part of the appropriation of forgiveness.

Secondly, because of this highly important role which the models and the theories constructed around them are seen to have in the mediation of the forgiveness wrought by Christ in his death, an interesting question could be raised about their comprehensiveness. Do they, in fact, cover the whole area of human sin and wrong-doing, all the points at which God may find the sinners for whom his forgiving grace is searching? This question is obviously not going to be given a categorical yea or nay answer. The grace of God is free, and like his Spirit bloweth where it listeth, and saves whom he will. Equally, there may one day be given to us a new model, as we said before, which answers to some expresion of human sin so far undetected. But the fact that the models with which we do operate have sustained the traffic of divine forgiveness across so many centuries creates an *a priori* impression of their near-completeness, if not their actual completeness.

Thirdly, since the terms in which the redeeming death of Christ is to be described are to be also the pathways that we variously follow at different times and in different cultures and societies, it becomes supremely important that these descriptions are offered, from the very start, as the basis for forgiveness. We dealt earlier critically with the proposition that there was no reason why God should not forgive sins by simply willing to do so. There is an extension of that proposition in the thought that God might simply forgive our sins in the immediacy of the I-Thou confrontation, without the mediation of the calvary story and the models in which it is interpreted. By implication, the rejection of the one proposition is the same as that applied to the other. The forgiveness which God offers is the sacrificial love, which is to be understood and appropriated only in the context of the death of Christ. So when we speak of 'the experience of forgiveness', we have always to remember that it is forgiveness experienced in the context of the sacrificial redeeming love of Jesus Christ, and that there is no short-cut to forgiveness which somehow thinks that it can achieved by some cheaper route.

Fourthly, as we move from discussion of the theology of atonement, and the components of soteriology to the actual ways in which atonement and redemption are implemented in the lives of men and women, we have moved into the realm of homily and pastoral care. Concerning the former, insofar as one of its purposes must be to bring to its hearers the grace of God in Jesus Christ and the forgiveness which flows therefrom, it is imperative that the preacher should build his/her presentation upon the whole foundation of salvation as we have been describing it. It is the whole Gospel which has to be preached, for it is the whole Gospel which saves. Concerning pastoral care, insofar as it involves direct or indirect counselling, the models of salvation offer a whole range of openings to an understanding of personal guilt, or alienation, or aggression, or defeatism, or whatever it is that is the cause of disorientation or plain unhappiness. But more, the models offer the variety of ways in which Jesus the Redeemer may meet the needs of his people.

IV.

If forgiveness may be said to have its foundation in the redeeming death of Jesus Christ, it achieves its goal, namely, the salvation of individual men and women of every age and race, through the efficacy of the contemporanisers, the universalisers and the relaters, which we examined in our fourth chapter. Through them, the one-time, one-place event of calvary transcends itself to refer to and to comprehend those for whose sake 'the Word was made flesh, and dwelt among us'. As we saw, the New Testament employed a range of prepositions which have yielded adjectival conceptualisations and the Church has developed its own media which together express particularity in the midst of generality, contemporaneity after two thousand years of history, total justification in face of righteous condemnation of all human sin. But if our construction of the shape of soteriology is to be complete, it remains for us to show how this particularity, contemporaneity and justification earth themselves in the soul of the sinner who lays claim upon the mercy of God for the forgiveness of his/her sins. Biblical and theological literature has many descriptions of how this earthing takes place. It came to Zacchaeus, when, in the presence of Christ, he became deeply aware of his dishonesty, and making amends in the only way he knew, found the salvation which God had prepared for those that are lost. (Lk 19.9). Nicodemus (Jo 3.3ff) learned of that same salvation in terms, with which we are still familiar, of being born again. Peter declared his awareness of this earthing, when he witnessed the power of Christ (Mt 16.16), and uttered his own confession, 'Thou art the Christ, the Son of he living God'. And so on to St Paul on the way to Damascus, to St Augustine and to the whole army of the saints down to our own time, who in one way or another learned that the Lamb slain before the foundation of the world had been slain for them.

The single inclusive term for the response to the unfolded story of what God has done in Jesus towards the redemption is 'faith', so familiar a term that we pass it over, in our haste to reach the next idea. But I propose to tarry a while with it, for it is in our response that the whole vast salvific purpose of God for each one of us reaches its sharpest point. There was a time when, in our study of psychology with Professor Drever of the University of Edinburgh, we learned of the three modes of consciousness - knowing or cognition, feeling or affection or emotion, and willing or conation or volition. The terms are fairly self-explanatory, and the claim made for them was that, at any one moment, a cross-section of our conscious life would involve our operating in all three modes. A brief pause in the proceedings for an opportunity of uninhibited self-analysis

will, I predict, reveal the *prima facie* truth of this account of
one part of our mental life. But it is when I apply this analysis
to the manner in which faith operates, that I find it most
illuminating and helpful. Let us follow the account through its
three elements. First, the cognitive component in faith consists
of its awareness of what we have been hitherto been deploying
in the description of the story of the cross and its several
interpretations. It would be wrong to pretend that that awareness is in any sense totally comprehensive, either in range or in
depth. In fact, nobody is ever going to achieve that level of
comprehension. Yet without some degree of understanding of
what God has done in Jesus Christ, then it difficult to see to
what faith is responding, or what it is that stimulates the
emotional elements in the response. Though St Paul at 1 Tim
1.12b was reflecting upon a more advanced stage of Christian
faith, when he said, 'I know whom I have believed', his words
would apply with obvious modifications to all stages of believ-
ing. When we use the phrase 'blind belief', we do not imply
that the believer is blind to the subject of belief, but rather to
the many contrary circumstances which, in the judgment of
others, count heavily against belief in that subject. As Barth
points out in his *Fides Quaerens Intellectum,* when comment-
ing upon St Anselm's famous statement, *'Credo ut intelligam'*
(I believe in order that I may understand), the theorem does
not work unless there has been prior awareness of the item of
faith concerned, what Barth calls 'the exterior text' to be read
and apprehended by believers and unbelievers alike.

Secondly, the affective mode of consciousness is also in play
in faith, in a variety of forms. Consciousness of the mercy of
God revealed through the redeeming death of Jesus Christ
must produce a range of reactions, such as, shame over the
wrong-doing which has its place in the whole sin of mankind
which brought about the death of Jesus, and revulsion against
the sin which has caused the shame, for far too often with our

own wrong-doing, we reverse the well-known saying, and hate the sinner (ourselves) and love the sin; repentance, which should be the sequel to the shame and the conviction of sin; love towards the Lord Jesus Christ, which I emphasise most pointedly, for as Presbyterians loving Jesus has not been a marked feature of our religious emotional life - we are so much better at faith, which defines, analyses, acknowledges, affirms and confesses; and a deep-felt longing which eagerly desires to have what is offered in redemption.

Thirdly, the conative, volitional mode expresses itself in the act of will to accept what is offered so freely and graciously by God in Jesus Christ. This act of will may take the form of explicit statement, 'I believe; help thou mine unbelief', which, recalling J.L. Austin, in *How to do Things with Words,* (ed. J.O. Urmson, Oxford, 1962), we shall call a 'performative', a verbal action. It will, perhaps more frequently, take the form of explicit decision, or active obedience, or categorical commitment to Jesus Christ. In the volitional act, the first step has been taken into that new life of fellowship with God in Jesus Christ which is the fulfilment of the whole purpose of the atonement.

Let us reflect, then, upon this analysis of the structure of faith and thereafter upon the place of faith as the 'earthing' of the whole redemptive process. First, it would be wrong to suggest that the order of the three modes of faith as described is prescriptive, and is to be followed on all occasions and under all circumstances. In fact, as was indicated earlier, the three modes of consciousness represent three elements in a cross-section of consciousness at any one time; and by implication, the same may be said of faith, that when it occurs, it evinces these three modes. Equally, however, at any one moment, one or other mode may be dominant. In parenthesis, it could be noted that whole theologies have been written in the conviction that one or other of the modes of faith has precedence. In some forms of intellectualist Protestantism, the cognitive emphasis rates high, insofar as great importance is attached to correct propositional affirmation. Schleiermacher might be taken as the example of emphasis upon the place of feeling in faith; while existentialism, in whatever form it has occurred in theology, has given pre-eminence to decision and volition. That same kind of selection of one mode in faith to the reduction of the other two will in its own way yield varying accounts of the character which the redeemed life will have.

Secondly, the greatest care has to be taken, when speaking of faith as response to God's redeeming work in Christ, not to turn faith itself into a work, which certainly was never an error committed by the Reformers themselves, though it has often been the trap into which their sometimes unenlightened followers have fallen. It is a mistake made by those who point to the doctrine of 'justification by faith', and argue that all that has happened is that 'faith' has been substituted for 'works'; whereas in fact the justification is accomplished in the work of Christ, and the role of faith is to appropriate that salvation. It is a point that has often been made, but I do wonder whether those who make it have faced all the consequences of saying it. What is intended by the rejection of the idea that faith is itself a work is that just as we had no part in the earlier stages of our redemption - as Aulen, following St Paul, would have said, 'It is all of God' - so even our response is also 'of God'. So the best way of stating the nature of faith as it responds to God's redemptive action in Christ is to ascribe it, as we have observed in the previous chapter, to the work of the Holy Spirit in the human soul. It is a quite extensive work. For the Spirit is to be thought of as going ahead to prepare the way for the acceptance of the offer of forgiveness, to be present in the act of will in which the believer participates in the redemptive work of Christ on his/her behalf, and thereafter to sustain them in the life of discipleship of Christ which is the implementation of that initial act of obedience to the Saviour. At Eph 1.13, St Paul speaks of those 'who have heard the word of truth, the gospel of salvation', and have believed in Christ being 'sealed with the promised Holy Spirit', as the one who brings the whole redemptive process to its fulfilment in the actual forgiveness and renewal of men and women.

Thirdly, it is not difficult, from this vantage-point, to see how readily the emphasis upon the idea that salvation is 'all of God', conjoined with the refinement of that idea into the special role of the Holy Spirit in the believer's appropriation of the salvation offered in Jesus Christ, led to the doctrine of predestination in one or other of its forms. For if the faith involved in the acceptance of Christ's redeeming grace is the gift of God through his Spirit, then it would certainly appear to follow that those who reject that offer of Christ's, or who in fact do not have the opportunity either to accept it or reject it, have been denied the gift of the Spirit. Continuing that same logic, since this gift of the Spirit can not itself be based upon some prior goodness of the person, for 'all have sinned and come short of the glory of God' (Rom 3.23), the decision to give the Spirit to some and not to others would seem to have arisen out of the depths of God's own being, in short from a decree predestinating the results known in human life.

But there is harshness to this logic which for all its rigour fails to persuade, and so even at this late point in our enquiry, we have to ask, 'Is there another way?' An interesting and original answer was once propounded by Barth, that election and rejection are terms wrongly applied to two classes of people, so designated because they are the subjects of the appropriate divine decrees, willed by God before the beginning of time. On the contrary, 'elected' and 'rejected' are terms whose primary application in Christian theology is to Jesus Christ, the One who was by name and by nature the Beloved Son of the Father, and the One also who, for us and for our salvation, was despised and rejected, his dereliction enshrined for all time in the words from the cross, 'My God! My God! Why hast thou forsaken me?' So, since Christ entered into his passion, assuming human nature, for the sins of the whole world, humanity itself is both elected and rejected. It was for this reason that Brunner, (Scottish Journal of Theology, Vol.4 No.2, p.133) not altogether without seriousness, suggested that according to Barth all that was required of human beings to be saved was that they should be created, thus participating in the elect/rejected humanity. That I would regard as caricature. But I would say, taking up one of Barth's options, that we are all elect/rejected, but that some of us by that same grace are drawn towards, or decide for, the elect focus of our new existence; while others who do not so choose remain within the rejected, because rejecting, focus. Agreed: we thus arrive back at the point of departure, where some decide for and some against Christ, some through the gift of the Spirit, some through lack of it. Faced now apparently with the same old problem, I can only say that I am sure of two things. One is that the person who accepts the salvation offered in Christ, so decides through no power of his/her own, but only through the indwelling power of God's Spirit - even when the decision came after intense struggle. 'I yet not I' is the essence of such decision. Perhaps it is wrong to turn what is a positive affirmation about those who accept Christ's offer into a negative assertion concerning those who do not. I am reminded of our Lord's words to Peter when he was unduly curious about the fate of another, 'What is that to thee? Follow thou me' (Jo 21.22). My other conviction is that because Jesus took the whole of human nature, and some of our more daring theologians wish to say, sinful human nature, then even those whom a previous generation placed in what you might call the dust-bin of damnation are wrongly so regarded; they too have the elect/reject status, even though they exist at the reject focus. It is the fact they too have the elect/

reject status which gives validity to every appeal of the evangelist to repent and be saved. This position can not be dismissed as universalism, because there is too much evidence in the world of continuing human rejection of Christ. But at the same time, it contains too much scepticism to allow me to endorse limited atonement, scepticism, that is, of a position which, to my mind, prematurely and with insufficient evidence, reconciles the damnation of so many with not only the love, but also the justice and the judgment, of God.

V.

We turn now, in conclusion, to a description of the nature of forgiveness which emerges thus as the final stage of a process which issues from the very nature of God himself, which is sacrificially costly, the cost being the death of the Beloved Son of the Father. The very word 'forgiveness' carries a double meaning, which often goes undetected, but which is recognised in the OED. It means both 'the action of forgiving' and 'the condition or fact of being forgiven', the former being illustrated in Psalm 130.4 'But there is forgiveness with thee, that thou mayest be feared'; and the latter in Ac 13.38 (St Paul preaching) 'through this man [Jesus Christ] forgiveness of sins is proclaimed'. The former sense of forgiveness - it might be thought of as 'forgivingness' - is what we have been discussing up-to-date: the origins of that forgiveness in God's purpose for his creatures who had rebelled against him, the implementing of that purpose in the life, death and resurrection of Jesus Christ, and the gift of the Holy Spirit to give effect to that forgiving purpose in the actual forgiving of, and acceptance of being forgiven by, actual men and women. The latter sense of forgiveness - which might be considered as 'forgivenness' - has, in its turn, a double application, on the one hand to the sins which have been committed, and on the other, to the men and women who have committed them. There is a preponderance of biblical texts referring to the former application, though the second is not without its examples. I propose that we begin with the former, and work into the latter. With that programme in mind, let me present a profile of forgiveness:

First, when our sins are said to be forgiven, in the context of the conditions which make it possible, several points are being made, of which the first is that these sins are wiped out, cancelled, and no longer held against us; and in the language of Is 1.18, though they be 'like scarlet, they shall be white as snow'. So, too, our guilt, which is the entail of the past appearing in the present, in anguish of conscience and alienation of spirit, is removed; health, wholeness, holiness and integrity of heart and mind and spirit are restored; and broken relationships with God and our fellows made good. In a way, therefore, one of the prime characteristics of forgiveness is that it can re-make the past, in the present and *for* the future. There are few theological statements which carry greater pastoral weight than that; and equally few things that we should be saying with greater frequency from the pulpit than that. And yet, even when we have been so explicit, it remains still to say that the consequences from past sin that last on into the present are not always removable, even when the sin itself has been forgiven; and to that extent the past is irreversible, often because it has already become part of the physical fabric of humanity or society. That realistic acknowledgment must also be part of the pastoral awareness.

Secondly, at the personal level, and in the primary reference, forgiveness is the restoration of fellowship with God, or if we use the notion that is gaining popularity, friendship with God. At the heart of that fellowship is acceptance by God, and as Paul Tillich so often said, acceptance of that acceptance. But while the acceptance specifies the status of the forgiven sinner, the friendship which is thus initiated calls for a whole range of sustaining activities - of prayer and worship, of daily dedicated and obedient discipleship, a continuing sensitivity to the fact that forgiveness has to be constantly saught and acceptance constantly acknowledged, and through all and in all, the entreaty that God should provide his Spirit as the only Lord and Giver of life, who will make such discipleship and friendship daily possibilities and realities. At this point the forgiving process, which began with the Lamb that was slain before the foundation of the world, has come to its fulfilment and fruition.

Thirdly, or has it? We are all familiar with our Lord's reply to Peter, when he asked how often he had to forgive his brother for sinning against him. Seven times? No, said Jesus, '.. not to seven times, but to seventy times seven' (Mt 18.21f). What we have not so far taken account of, in all our deliberations, is the role which we as brothers and sisters play in the mediation of forgiveness to those about us. Two points: first, by refusing to forgive, we may actually be preventing the forgiveness of God from reaching others, and so bringing the purposes of God to frustration. Secondly, if we do not forgive those who have offended us, we shall not ourselves know forgiveness (Mt 18.23-35). No account of the shape of soteriology, however otherwise impeccable, can afford to ignore the final finishing touch thus given to it by human agency.

INDEX OF SUBJECTS

INDEX OF NAMES

INDEX OF BIBLICAL TEXTS